HOW TO DISAPPEAR COMPLETELY

On Modern Anorexia

HOW TO
DISAPPEAR
COMPLETELY

On Modern Anorexia

KELSEY OSGOOD

OVERLOOK DUCKWORTH

NEW YORK • LONDON

This edition first published in hardcover in the United States and the United Kingdom in 2013 by Overlook Duckworth, Peter Mayer Publishers, Inc.

NEW YORK
141 Wooster Street
New York, NY 10012
www.overlookpress.com
For bulk and special sales, please contact sales@overlookny.com,
or write us at above address.

LONDON
90-93 Cowcross Street
London EC1M 6BF
info@duckworth-publishers.co.uk
www.ducknet.co.uk
For bulk and special sales, please contact sales@duckworth-publishers.co.uk,
or write us at the above address.

Cataloging-in-Publication Data is available from the Library of Congress.
A catalogue record for this book is available from the British Library.

Design and typeformatting by Bernard Schleifer
Manufactured in the United States of America
ISBN 978-1-4683-0668-2 (US)
ISBN 978-0-7156-4753-0 (UK)
FIRST EDITION
1 3 5 7 9 10 8 6 4 2

For Henna and Kayla

And also my family
whose sheer perfection, every day, becomes clearer to me

Some names and attributes of characters in this book have been changed to protect the individuals' privacy.

CONTENTS

PROLOGUE 13

CHAPTER 1 The Beginning 17

CHAPTER 2 A Communicable Disease 25

CHAPTER 3 The Protagonist 39

CHAPTER 4 Idol Worship 53

CHAPTER 5 The Anorexia Spectrum 77

CHAPTER 6 Blurry Lines 105

CHAPTER 7 Titillation 131

CHAPTER 8 Plateau/Climax 147

CHAPTER 9 Hospitals 173

CHAPTER 10 Distances from Death 199

CHAPTER 11 Attempting Narrative 211

CHAPTER 12 The End 231

ACKNOWLEDGMENTS 259

SELECTED BIBLIOGRAPHY 263

Possible attitudes found in books 1) I don't know what's happening to me 2) what does it mean? 3) seized with the deepest sadness, I know not why 4) I am lost, my head whirls, I know not where I am 5) I lose myself 6) I ask you, what have I come to? 7) I no longer know where I am, what is this country? 8) Had I fallen from the skies, I could not be more giddy 9) a mixture of pleasure and confusion, that is my state 10) where am I, and when will this end? 11) what shall I do? I do not know where I am

—DONALD BARTHELME, "Alice"

When it's in a book, I don't think it'll hurt anymore . . . exist anymore. One of the things writing does is wipe things out. Replace them.

—MARGUERITE DURAS, *The Lover*

HOW TO DISAPPEAR COMPLETELY

On Modern Anorexia

PROLOGUE

WHEN THEY WHEELED THIRTY-TWO-YEAR-OLD ANNALISE'S stretcher onto the unit, the patients stood along the hallway walls and tried not to gape.

"Now *that's* a lesson in moderation," someone said.

I wasn't there when she was admitted. I was still enrolled in college, spending most of my time hiding from my watchful roommates and trying to rid myself of my last vice, sugared bubblegum. When I arrived a month after her admission, a younger patient told me about Annalise's first day, about how all the unit's inhabitants had quieted in horror at her presence. She stayed in her bed by order of the doctor the entire month I was a patient there. Occasionally, she would get a phone call and a nurse would wheel her out of her bedroom and down the corridor. She would lift the phone off the receiver and dial with the ends of her long yellow fingernails, the nails of a Chinese aristocrat of old, ones belonging to idle hands. She spoke only to her mother, and her voice was a weak croak. When I walked by her room, I would peek in and smile hello, fascinated by the disgusting creature who so rarely exited her bed. Eventually, we got to talking and she told me about how she was admitted to the hospital this time.

"I told my mother, 'Okay, you can call 911.'" Her eyes rolled and she smirked, revealing holes where teeth ought to have been. She lifted up her arm to show me her biceps, where doctors had inserted nineteen bags of IV fluid. Her skin was covered in stretch marks, jaundiced and flaky. The room stank of dead cells. Her hair was so severely dreadlocked that the staff had been forced to chop it off. She emerged from the bathroom a cadaver with a pageboy coif. I think about all the images of Annalise that together complete her pitiful, humiliating montage: the staff wheeling her into the bathroom, me watching and knowing that inside they would hold her over a pot while she tried in vain to shit, her whimpering about the amount of apple juice she was forced to drink.

"The juice is always really hard for me."

Her first steps down the hallway on rangy, atrophied legs, her terror at the prospect of being tube-fed. When the lawyers for patient rights came to visit, she requested a meeting. Two lawyers sat by the pay phones with Annalise as she looked at the papers. The lawyers turned the sheets for her one by one, and I imagined the spectacle of her in court, arguing to a judge that she knew better than the hospital did, that she could do it on her own, really. How could the judge not laugh in her face?

She told me she liked children, and I thought that kids would probably cross the street when they saw her. They would point and stare and make brazen comments to the adult that held their hands.

"Mommy, what's wrong with that lady?"

She was the worst, and perhaps most successful, anorexic I had ever seen.

"One in ten anorexics will die from the disease," a therapist had said when I was first hospitalized, three years before I met Annalise. "Look around the room. At least one of you will not make it."

I googled Annalise periodically after I left New York Presbyterian Westchester Hospital that time, as I did with many of the people I met in treatment. After nearly eight years of googling with no results, one day I stumbled upon her death notice on a funeral home website. Someone wrote that she had passed away after a "long and courageous battle." There was a picture of her in the "Slide Show of Memories," and though she was only forty in it, she looked closer to seventy. Her cheeks were full and chipmunkish, but her jugular was oddly pronounced and her closed-mouth smile awkward and sunken, betraying her lack of teeth. It was the only picture in the slide show, and it remained on the screen as a Muzak version of "Amazing Grace" played on repeat.

CHAPTER 1

THE BEGINNING

In the summer of 1998, when I was fourteen years old, I spent my days at a bookstore near my house. I was bored and eager to escape our stuffy, un-air-conditioned house in the few weeks between camp and family vacation, so I would ride my shiny teal bicycle down to the small shopping area, park out front, and spend an hour or so browsing the bookshelves. I had always been a bookworm, or at least that's what people said about me. "She *loves* to read."

I was small for my age, a girl with a china-doll face and blond hair cut into a straight bob, and I probably looked quite darling with my head buried in a big, fat bound text. Sometimes I developed grand, inexplicable literary ambitions, such as when I decided I would read *Les Misérables* at age eight, or *Anne of Green Gables* for my first fourth-grade book report. When my teacher gently suggested I pick something else due to time constraints, I broke down in tears right there in the library of my elementary school. I read everything I could get my hands on, from Roald Dahl to the diary of Anne Frank to science-fiction stories. When I visited the school library, I would wander up and down the aisles and brush my fingertips over the cracked spines of the books, marveling at the number of stories there were in the world, eager for the time when I would be smart and old enough to write my own.

These summer expeditions were different, though. More focused, as I had a specific subject of study to attack. I would stand on trembling legs, slick with cold sweat, and scan the psychology section. It wasn't a particularly well-stocked establishment, but there were still many books about young people, mostly girls, who felt crazy, or *were* crazy. I didn't think I was crazy, but I kind of wished I were. Crazy people were privy to a universal truth, I thought, destined for artistic greatness, their words indelibly scalded into the collective conscious. And even if they weren't mad geniuses, only drooling, voiceless fools, at least they could opt out of regular life. At that time, the idea of taking up residence in a state mental hospital didn't seem entirely unappealing to me, though I had no personal reference for what that kind of place was like and therefore no basis for making such a judgment. Becoming a professional patient, a "hopeless case," seemed akin to selling one's possessions and dropping out to live on a commune or defecting to Canyon Ranch for a long-term detox. And besides, most of the "hopeless cases" I read about actually ended up confounding the doctors' prognoses, recovering and then writing books, so what were a few years lost to psychosis if you ended up a famous author at the other end? If I were actually crazy, I would be allowed to exit, at least for a while, the *real* world, a place I found at once deeply overwhelming and utterly lacking. I wouldn't have to do all the things that I had always considered pointless, like take math tests or sit up straight or tell white lies. I wouldn't have to be what I thought I was: short, stumpy, decidedly unglamorous, not outstanding in any particular way. Normal. Or maybe nothing at all.

My opinion of myself had crumbled over the past two years. I felt awkward in my body and my persona. I had read the pamphlets and seen the movies they showed us after school, and so I knew that there was a reasonable biological explanation for all of this awkwardness, and that was puberty. I knew that all those changes in my body, the lumps and hairs and hot smells, were affecting my brain. I had already read *Reviving Ophelia: Saving the Selves of Adolescent Girls,* the 1994 classic by clinical psychologist Mary Pipher about the horrors of being a teenager and female. It didn't matter to me; this awful anachronistic feeling must be remedied somehow if I was to survive high school. There had to be a way to get through it. And one day it dawned on me: I was fat.

"But it couldn't have been that simple," one might protest. Oh, but it was. It was a specific moment, too. I was thirteen years old, had just switched from public to private school, and was out to lunch with my old classmates. We went to an Italian restaurant, where they ordered salads and I ordered pizza. As we walked around the one street that comprised our suburb's downtown area, my stomach churned with cheese and confusion. I felt suddenly that I didn't belong anywhere, that I was strange and without purpose; inside flew about those typical teenage emotions that felt, to me, entirely new, potent, and completely debilitating. I looked down at my stomach. It protruded. I sucked it in, then let it out again. I jabbed my belly with my pointer finger and announced to one of my friends, "I'm fat."

"No, you're not," she said. I didn't think she was very fervid, so I tried again.

"My stomach is huge."

"Just do some sit-ups," Arianna said, tossing her thick brown hair over her shoulder. I didn't think this reply was a negation. A train rumbled on the tracks nearby.

So that was it: I was fat, and I would get thin. Adolescent girls were always supposed to be worrying about such things, weren't they? And so I did. I worried. Later that night, in the solitude of my dim bedroom, I pinched my upper arms and deemed them sausage-like. I slapped the flesh of my thighs and watched them jiggle and squeezed tears from my eyes. Had everyone seen this but me? How could I have failed to notice this earlier?

And if I was going to get thin, I might as well get *really* thin, right? I might as well throw everything I had into it. I might as well become the thinnest of all.

In hindsight I can say that no, I was not fat. I was not a natural waif, but I wasn't *fat* or even chubby, really. My baby layers remained around my stomach and midsection, but the rest of me was solid flesh, finely proportioned. Normal, but then again, that may have been the point.

At public school, most of us had known one another since early childhood. I knew what adjectives my peers would have used to describe me: small, smart, sarcastic, good at spelling, a decent singer and actress. At my new school, a prestigious kindergarten through 12th grade private school housed in an old Rockefeller mansion, I felt borderline transparent: not unpopular or maligned, but not distinct in any way. Mediocre. Next year I would be a freshman, but what sort of freshman would I be? Every high school had to have its *Girl, Interrupted,* its token baby-carrot eater. I had always been sad, inclined toward morbid subjects, so why not give my sadness a goal? I would get so thin that I would be the physical embodiment of sadness, and there would be not a flicker of doubt in the universe that I was exactly that: thin and sad. I would be consumed and ravaged by thinness, by the pursuit of it. I wished for this the way other girls craved a cool boyfriend or the latest designer handbag. The designer handbag wouldn't have been enough for me, I knew from experience, and a boyfriend was out of the question. I didn't think I was unattractive, but rather that I had begun a slow descent into ugliness, that my three- and four-year-old eerily doll-looking self was as pretty as I'd ever be. I was already convinced of my lack of value as a sexual object by the fifth grade, when I wouldn't even write the name of my crushes down in my diary because God would know my audacity. By eighth grade, I wasn't writing in a diary anymore, or thinking that an omniscient power was reading my private thoughts over my shoulder, but I had come to believe with certitude that I was unattractive. No boy would ever want my small chest, thick thighs, hairy arms, or dwarf stature. Even if one did, I suspected it would have been just a shade more satisfying than getting the new Kate Spade purse. I didn't need something to have; I needed something to *be*.

It never occurred to me to try to lose weight in any healthy way, or to strive for a body that "looked good." I wanted to be repulsively thin, and I knew how people got that way, and that was by being anorexic. I didn't think of anorexia as a disease, really, but rather as the most logical progression of self-control. It was dieting perfected, and perfection was always the goal. Determination was a quality I had always considered myself particularly deficient in, discipline, too, but all that would change. If I were going to learn to make poetry, it would be by imitating Sylvia Plath.

My eyes scanned the titles of the books in the little store by my house, many of which I'd at least skimmed by then. I saw *When Food's a Foe,* by therapist Nancy Kolodny. I had read it earlier that summer, concentrating mostly on the personal accounts and patient profiles. I recalled reading a quote in it from a girl named "Felicity," a patient Kolodny had interviewed for the book. "I heard my parents talking about how my therapist had said I wasn't that bad," Felicity said. "Well, I'll get there. *I'll show them.*" I thought of this kindred spirit often and wondered where she was in her quest. I passed over *I Never Promised You a*

Rose Garden and *Sybil* and *The Quiet Room,* fondly recalling each schizophrenic or otherwise insane protagonist as if she were a dear confidante and friend. There were the anorexia books I had already read: *Second Star to the Right,* by Deborah Hautzig, and of course, Steven Levenkron's *The Best Little Girl in the World.* The latter was every anorexic of my generation's entrée into the world of eating disorders literature. I had borrowed the book from a friend of a friend, and had to be repeatedly asked to return it. Published in 1978, Levenkron's book was one of the earliest fictional accounts of anorexia, and its main character was a Manhattan high-schooler named Francesca Dietrich. She was a perfectionist *and* a ballerina—a double threat. Francesca, or Kessa, as she began calling herself when she started dieting, was a composite character of all the patients Levenkron had ever treated, replete with symptoms and obsessions and health scares. She gave herself a new identity with her eating disorder, a new name. Francesca became Kessa, the indomitable dieter. *This is what I can do for you,* the illness said through her. *I can make you new.*

Finally, my eyes rested on *Wasted,* subtitled *A Memoir of Anorexia and Bulimia.* Author Marya Hornbacher was pictured on the cover wearing understated clothing and a serious expression. Face their audience, she and Elizabeth Wurtzel, wunderkind author of *Prozac Nation,* did, both pouting prodigies with slack-lidded, come-hither eyes, the offspring of heroin chic and girl power, without the pesky criminal records.

I bought the book and devoured it, of course. Hornbacher wove her tale of grape meals and cardiac symptoms with such artistry as to make me swoon at the prospect of such success. Without a doubt, she was thin, and that's what I wanted, too, *without a doubt,* the body relentlessly diminished, the story violently constricted and simplified. After reading it, I incorporated some of Hornbacher's tricks into my own weight-loss repertoire. She was my hero, a near-impossible ideal of self-denial. For quite some time, I considered myself to be an anomaly at best and a despicable phony at worst, for if I were really "eating disordered," wouldn't I despise food outright? Wouldn't starvation have come to me naturally? If I were a "real" anorexic, wouldn't it have been silently and divinely inspired and not something I sought consciously as a means to salvation?

CHAPTER 2

A COMMUNICABLE DISEASE

UNTIL ABOUT AGE TWENTY-THREE, I WAS PROUD TO HAVE been anorexic. I could speak at length about my illness with nearly anyone. But now, when faced with the dreaded "What is your book *about?*" I shift in my chair and wax existential about America's cult of dramatization. I talk about diagnostic drift and relate it to the rapid rise in autism, the establishment of such bizarre and universally applicable mental maladies as depersonalization disorder, characterized by "dissociation from the self." I even touch upon the Internet and the death of communication and the fact that maybe one day, yes, I think we will all have Avatars and Second Lives and *Third* Lives, and nothing will be considered real until we blog about it, until it is observed by another. But if the listener waits patiently, I inevitably forge a little deeper into the forest, revealing that I once had anorexia, and how I have always noticed in myself and my peers, both eating disordered and not, a peculiar and disturbing trend: many of us would seek out materials aimed at eating disorder "awareness" and prevention and use them instead as instruction manuals, often banding together to collaborate on our great demises. One can recognize flickers of this aspirational phenomenon in the high school cafeteria by watching the girls who want to diet glance furtively at the token anorexic as she strategically picks at a muffin. No teenage girl is a stranger to the idea of pacts made by members of cliques to eat only x and y until prom, sometimes with titles as brazen as "Plan Anorexia." That striving is apparent in more acute forms in therapists' waiting rooms or hospital group sessions: patients with sunken eyes whispering to the person in front of them in line for the bathroom, "Just tell me what you weigh . . . *c'mon*," or on the Internet pages of "wannarexics," girls who give themselves screen names like 22TinyTina and Dying2BThin and post entries that read, *I need a REAL ana buddy. not someone that i talk to once. someone who will make a bet/competition with me and we check on eat* [sic?] *other every day to see how the other one is doing. like someone who is realllly interested in this.*

Anorexia is contagious, I explain to other writers and curious friends. It is a behavior that can be learned *through* stories. It doesn't necessarily develop organically or arise in the unknowing adolescent like the hysterical religious fervor of the "fasting girls" of yore. Not anymore, at least. One can study hard and ace the test. Joan Jacobs Brumberg, a professor at Cornell University and author of the very informative and unsentimental history of the disease *Fasting Girls,* theorizes in the introduction to another book on the topic that after the death of thirty-two-year-old Karen Carpenter in 1983, anorexia became better known to society at large, which led to an onslaught of depictions of the disease in magazine articles, novels, memoirs, and television movies. Some of the works were meant as cautionary tales, she writes, while others, perhaps unexpectedly, became "how-to" guides. "Today," she concludes, "many assert that the Internet plays a role in the 'communicability' of eating disorders."

Communicable, like herpes, mumps, AIDS, or the flu. Defined in *Webster's Third New International Dictionary* as:

1. Capability of being communicated—a) imparted without undue difficulty, b) transmitted from one to another, or

2. Talkative, open or frank rather than taciturn; given to communicating.

A vast amount of material on the subject, including but not limited to memoirs, is instructive for the reader, and the writer is probably aware of this, and getting something out of it him or herself. For anorexics, even those in recovery, the narrative toward rock bottom is more often than not a "war story" told to impress the listener, something that would be decried in almost any therapeutic environment as pernicious or, at best, just unnecessary. Even when someone eating disordered has recovered, he or she still retains an attachment to the anorexic value system. The lowest weight one reached remains a point of pride, not of shame, and it's rarely a self-less act to lay out the nitty-gritty of one's diet. Nine times out of ten, writing about anorexia beguiles at-risk populations for all the wrong reasons, and the person writing about his or her own struggle fuels the fire by producing a long, hubristic poem, an elegy, an ode to a presence gone and missed. An homage. The writers know they're up at the invisible podium to speak out about their journey to the brink of death (oh, yeah, and back) and they know, too, that the ones listening the closest are the young ones eager to enlist in the starving armies. They know that stories from the trenches, tales of walking, talking cadavers with skin like rice paper, will probably be used as incentive to lose a few inches off the waist, and the idiosyncrasies of their prison-esque diets will likely be little more than the basis for self-imposed meal plans. Maybe they themselves once were the listeners, mining any story for inspiration to starve better. And yet they commit their narratives to paper and allow them to be published and distributed.

Add to this that we live in an age that places an increasing premium on the sharing of one's story and, in a subversive and often ignored way, values most those who have stories that are scary, controversial, and redemptive. Memoir, as an example of this cultural hunger for the personal narrative, is one of the fastest growing genres of literature. According to Ben Yagoda, author of *Memoir: A History*, total sales of memoirs increased more than 400 percent between 2004 and 2008. The memoir that depicts a tragic life has become so popular that it has spawned its own subgenre, commonly referred to as the misery memoir. The more horrifying one's tale, the better the book sells. The Internet has also allowed us to make public our tiniest thoughts and actions, and has increased our large cultural reliance on the act of confession for confession's sake. We're moving closer to that brave new world in which nothing exists until it is splayed open for all to see and judge, and this includes eating disorders. As a result, girls can, and do, take to the Internet to detail their starvation diets, brag about their weight loss, or point like-minded, faceless "friends" in the direction of books rife with starvation tips or lists of malnutrition symptoms (you know, in case you want to be sure you're *succeeding*). This is a disembodied culture of people conspiring on how to kill themselves and one another, many smirking as they do it, getting as high off the collaborative aspect of it as they do from the starvation or disordered eating itself.

This phenomenon isn't always shocking to those who listen as I outline my thesis. Many of them are members of my peer group, decried as the Me Generation, and thus have either struggled with addictive behaviors themselves or known intimately someone who has. Most know the lexicon of rehab, "the hospital," wilderness programs for wayward youths. They know that "CO" means "constant observation" and that seventy-two hours is the maximum amount of time you can be legally detained on a unit if you're over eighteen and not determined to be a danger to yourself. Many know the milieu personally, and these people's ears prick up when I mention the conspiratorial air of the fucked up, the attention these populations often give to their literary canon, the collective sizing-up of the New Kid on the Eighth Floor: "What's *she* in for?" The question meaning, of course, "What kind of threat does she pose to me and my identity as a disturbed individual?" But these people are not all eating disordered; in fact, many attest to having noticed this contesting inclination in non-eating-disordered populations. Adults in rehab for narcotics abuse, kids who go to Al-Anon, counselors tasked to accompany angry adolescents up a mountain trail: even they, sometimes, get a buzz off the tragedy and its one-upmanship. "Oh, yeah? Well, get a load of *my* story!"

Part of this phenomenon is inherently human. We all want to be validated and feel that our travails matter to others. But this competitive strain has a special hold over anorexics, who measure their self-worth by determining how severe and "successful" their starvation is, and who often become increasingly caught up in the rivaling aspects of the illness as they become sicker and their brains, compromised by lack of nutrition, start to operate more frequently on obsessive loops. Sadly, when an anorexic enters a treatment environment, it can often just make the whole cycle worse—the more competitive the climate, the more motivation the anorexic feels to "succeed" by becoming sicker, and the sicker the anorexic becomes, the more likely he or she is to see competition everywhere.

Why is anorexia such a competitive illness? There are many reasons. For starters, anorexia is often the sufferer's loud declaration that he or she is different from other people.

It's what makes me special is a sentence that can be found in almost any firsthand testimonial about an eating disorder. The illness becomes a badge of uniqueness, often the only thing of value the sufferer believes he or she has. (I write this not to negate the real pain that anorexics go through, but to point out that belief in anorexia's importance to one's identity is a hallmark of the illness.) The anorexic's goal isn't to diet normally, but rather to diet *profoundly*—to diet better than anyone in the world, particularly other pro dieters. Alcoholics, as a point of contrast, are often dismayed that they cannot drink like people who are not alcoholics. This is obviously not true of all alcoholics, as not every symptom of a problem occurs in every diseased person, but the general pathology is outlined in the bible of the 12-Step group *Alcoholics Anonymous,* otherwise known as the Big Book. "No person," it's written therein, "likes to admit he is bodily and mentally different from his fellows. Therefore, it is not surprising that our drinking careers have been characterized by countless vain attempts to prove we could drink like other people." More often than not, anorexics don't see their refusal to eat like non-eating-disordered people as a source of embarrassment; they see it as a source of pride.

"Think of anorexia as the negative marathon of eating disorders," writes Jessica Reaves in *Time* magazine. Everyone is sprinting around the track, eager to win. Knowing that someone is a few yards ahead of you, for some runners, is the fuel that makes your feet fly.

But anorexia is serious, an illness not devoid of meaning in health or metaphor. It is a condition that has gripped us visually and philosophically ever since it became recognized in popular culture in the late 1960s, despite the fact that it had existed as a diagnosis since the 1870s, when the hot debate over whether or not fasting girls possessed magical powers bequeathed by God still raged. Silence and ignorance are not acceptable in the face of such a monster, either. So we must ask ourselves: will any attempt to shed some light on this strange and cannibalistic disorder only make it worse? Has examining and writing about anorexia accomplished nothing? Are all the writers self-serving sensationalists, or simply naive? Or did they just choose the wrong words, the worst details, and package their stories poorly? Seductively, even?

When I visit Barnes & Noble's website and type "anorexia" into the search box, more than 459 results pop up. The category is almost equally split between memoirs and educational texts, with a few novels thrown in, most of these cross-categorized as young-adult books. The intensely visual nature of the disease is used to the advantage of the book vendors in ways that may or may not be demonizing or transparent or straightforward or all of these things. The memoirs are usually subtitled, the main title a short, angst-draped zinger (*Wasted, Empty, Stick Figure, Perfect)*, the subtitle a minor elaboration on this theme, indicating whether the narrative will focus on the happy restitution, on hope (*A Diary of Anorexia and Recovery, A Mother and Daughter's Triumph Over Teenage Eating Disorders)* or the actual progression of the illness itself (*A Diary of My Former Self, A Story of Anorexia, A Memoir of Anorexia and*

Bulimia). The second category, if only through omission, acknowledges its reality: that the meat of the story, ironically,
is in the bad behavior, the avalanche of grief, as opposed to
the stabilization, which is less narratively riveting. While the
former might appeal more to those who are not suffering
(friends and family members of anorexics want to read
about recovery), the latter appeals directly to those with a
vested interest in the voyeuristic exploration of anorexia:
those suffering and those who wish to suffer, like I did once
upon a time.

In my state of relative health and maturity, I often
think about these "angst-draped zingers." It's a fairly awkward phrase meant to highlight the fact that these adjectives
connote an attractive sort of negative—black, thick velvet
to those readers who are (or wish to be) shivering all the
time. To write these words in sixteen-point type and slap
them on the cover of the book is to market it toward people
who feel that way or want to or are: perfect, empty, wasted.
This is a standard approach to reaching a target audience;
it's unfortunate that the demographic, in this case, will gar-
ner self-destructive inspiration from the book they buy and
then consume, sometimes consciously and of their own accord.
This is the major difference between memoirs of anorexia
and bulimia and memoirs of other addictions: rarely, if ever,
will a heroin addict, sick or recovering, seek out a memoir
of drug addiction in order to learn how to become a *better*
practicing addict. An alcoholic generally doesn't read *Drinking: A Love Story* in an attempt to beef up his or her alcoholic repertoire by learning new clever ways to disguise

being plastered. Even rarer would be the healthy person who reads those books to directly learn how to develop a problem. A rebellious teenager would not typically turn toward *Loose Girl: A Story of Promiscuity* for advice on becoming sexually compulsive.

The more obvious problem with books on anorexia, and the one more easily remedied, is the aesthetic one. Almost all the memoirs, and even a vast majority of the other eating-disorder-related texts, sport jackets that feature too-slender girls, silhouettes of long, thin bodies and long, thin hair. Occasionally the girl is alone; sometimes she is next to her fat spectral counterpart. There are a few too many shots of bare, bony backs. All very "thinspiring," to use the rhetoric of today's ambitious students of anorexia. It is nothing short of sickening that in these books, the protagonists often salivate over fashion magazines splashed with pictures of bodies that look as underfed as their anorexic ones, and while the fashion magazines are decried as corrosive to young girls' self-esteem, these books, with their visual aids and their prescriptive content, are seen as the products of courage, rigorous honesty, and personal triumph.

The idea behind these covers is clearly to conjure the effect of a fun-house mirror, but the photographers have it all wrong. If they had truly wanted to represent anorexia in an image, they would have distorted the girl's body the other way by making her squat and wide. They would have shown a body lumpy and disproportionate: plump arms with a jutting collarbone or a pregnant-looking belly and blue fingernails. They would have shown the way anorexia makes the protagonist *feel*: deformed, freakish, swathed in layers of protective clothing, bulges in some places, bones in another. There ought to be no model in a black-and-white print, no heavily-lined doe eyes and wistful facial expression, just a round, neutered creature, or better yet, solid black, something unifying and communist that completely erases the body and the individual within it as opposed to spotlighting it.

Am I saying that anorexia would cease to exist if people didn't write or talk about it? That it would disappear if we gave it the cultural silent treatment? Of course not. Kafka's fictional Hunger Artist regaled Europe with his public fasting but continued to starve himself long after the peanut-crunching crowd had moved on to witness the animals, in the end dying quietly and without fanfare. But the growth of the pro-ana movement, the vague online-based effort to recast anorexia as a "lifestyle choice," among other things, the ubiquity of memoirs about starving and vomiting and running and running and running, and the increasing prevalence of diagnosable eating disorders: all these things have occurred within the past thirty years. Awareness must, therefore, play a role, but it's not the only factor. It's the *way* in which we talk about eating disorders. There has to be a way to do so productively, to shift the language we use, to defy the conventions of the narrative so that prospective anorexics are repelled and not drawn to the idea of illness.

And so I decided, at twenty-six: I will write a book about anorexia without ever once recording someone's weight. It can be done. After all, as an anorexic, I could never really possess my lowest weight. When I saw it on the scale, it was a lie, or I had ingested some water before. I was wearing jeans, which added a few pounds, or I had taken laxatives last night so it was an underestimate, or it was down and I was elated, but only for a moment until the inevitable evil machinations began: *Well, if* this *feels good, imagine what a lower weight would feel like!* I never got to own my nadir.

In 2000, the first of four times I was hospitalized, a nurse wrote my weight on a tiny piece of paper and slipped it to me, as I was not supposed to know it. I don't know why she agreed to tell me when I asked her. I showed the paper to my curious friends and watched for their reactions. One girl said, "My goodness, that's low!" And then I felt it, for a moment, that feeling that this was *really* happening and I was thin *without a doubt,* but then I stuffed the paper in my pocket and repeated the numbers in my head over and over again until they floated up, buoyant, lost to me forever.

I will never disclose how many calories I ate in a day. In fact, I never *really* knew. In high school, I used to sit in trigonometry class and calculate my intake obsessively in the margins of my notebook, each time coming up with the same answer, each time dismissing my mathematics as unreliable. "You have to do it again. You have to be *sure.*" The reader will want to know all these gory details—what *did* she eat in a day? What were her safe foods?—of this I am certain. But if I were to lay it all out, clearly and concisely, I would be rendering an inaccurate portrait, making my disease seem tangible and solid when really the experience of it is deviously ephemeral.

By withholding the salacious—the numbers, essentially—I will attempt to show the bloody blue innards of the monster as opposed to its gleaming, sharp fangs or elegant black cloak. To reveal it as messy and disgusting and awkward and sad and pathetic. Because I know, now, that the only way to understand anorexia, its magnetism on both a large and a small scale, and how to beat it, is to examine and then devalue its currency. It's to strip it bare of its beautiful language and its glamorous, deathly aura. Luckily, its currency is simple and defined, and therefore our task is easier.

CHAPTER 3

THE PROTAGONIST

WHERE I AM FROM EVERYTHING IS PRETTY. DRIVEWAYS lined with perfectly curved trees lead to houses that sit on cushy green lawns. The train station is just far enough away that the houses don't rattle with each passing engine but close enough that we can hear their faint rumblings in the middle of our darkest nights. In the mornings, these trains carry our fathers, who wear well-tailored suits and read the morning paper, off to the city, returning them back home at night. Our mothers are thinner than our teenagers because they play tennis during the day. In the summertime, we go to country clubs, larger houses that sport even more expansive, even cushier green lawns. There the children take golf and swimming lessons and acquire that perfect summer look: hair slightly chlorine green, freckles born of the sun on their noses and cheeks, sweet browned arms muscled from laps of freestyle and repetitions of backhand. Even our dogs are handsome, fit, and well-groomed, with shiny, lustrous coats made for television screens.

All this beauty confused me as a child. *Because life, really, is very, very ugly,* I thought. *Isn't it?*

My house had a two-acre yard with a swing set and a dilapidated barn and a stream we waded through in search of the ever-elusive suburban frog, but none of these things seemed more alluring than the small graveyard across the street. The names on the headstones threw me into the whirl of an imaginative tornado. Who was she, this Emily Walker, who died when she was forty-six years old? How did she go? What did she *feel?* The stones with slanted edges, traces of names or initials often wiped away by harsh New England winds over the past century. Who was buried beneath them? A child, an infant, a beloved family pet? If you sat in the graveyard at night, could you hear them, these day-silent creatures, whispering to one another? Had they left anything behind at all?

Death always seemed more romantic than well-decorated living rooms.

I used the set of encyclopedias my parents gave me to study Sylvia Plath, Biafran babies, Charles Manson, and Nostradamus. Presumably I looked up other things, but these are the ones I remember, particularly the image of an emaciated baby's distended belly and the mention of Sylvia Plath's "horror of childbirth." I fixated on Nostradamus's predictions, particularly the one that said the world would end in the year 2000. I would be sixteen that year. This kept me awake at night. I tried to imagine what people are like when they are sixteen. It sounded like a wondrous age, a joyride year, either the perfect time to die or the worst, I couldn't decide. I talked about the seer and his prophecy on the school bus incessantly. My friends would turn away, disturbed, not yet old enough to know how to change the subject, and even though I sensed their discomfort, I couldn't stop talking about it.

None of these dark fascinations made sense, really, because I was a beautiful child who lived in a beautiful house and had beautiful parents. Our Christmas cards were spectacular, with my two younger brothers and I dressed up in matching plaid outfits, our white-blond hair shining like the sun off metal. Adults would tell my mother I was cute while I was standing there, in that way adults do. But I wasn't cute. I wasn't cute at all. I liked ugly things. I was ugly.

And years later, beginning the fits-and-spurts process of writing this book, I put down, "I don't really care that I hurt myself anymore because sadness is beautiful, isn't it?"

So maybe that. Maybe I was beautiful, or I wanted to be. Maybe I even used the word "beautiful" then, in my head. I told my piano teacher I liked songs in minor keys better than those in major keys because they sounded graceful. Haunting, fragile, like the thinnest glass. I never wanted to play a scherzo.

A lapse, now, into a defense of my caretakers that I'm sure will come off as the lady protesting too much. The goal of therapy has always been, to some degree, to discover what it was *in your childhood* that made you feel one awful

way or another. "They fuck you up, your mum and dad,"
Philip Larkin's infamous poem "This Be the Verse" begins.
Even as we've moved away from reliance on the idea of refrigerator moms and oedipal complexes, we still believe that
the seeds of sadness are sown in childhood, and these giants
of our youth, then, must play large roles in our developing
depression or other mental instabilities. I don't think this is
entirely true for me. My parents steered the course of my
development, but the bad behavior I later cultivated was not
so much a reaction to them as a result of the way I felt my
own personality—morbid, self-indulgent, and incessantly
reflective—compared to what I perceived as theirs—
even-keeled, well-adjusted, and happy. Another idea: I was
a predictably precocious child and I knew the abominable
aspects of the society I inhabited. I knew its stereotypical inhabitants were apt to be superficial, cold, and narrow-
minded. I knew that I was inheriting a tradition of keeping-
up-appearances, and I fucking hated my ancestry, on theory,
and I hated my parents, to an extent, for keeping up their
own appearances, which were always well-coiffed and
diplomatic. My mother donned dresses that perfectly fit her
trim frame and kept her hair in a brown bob that fell just
below her ears. She was consummately proper and had always been that way. She had been the perfect child, she often
told me, and when I balked at this outrageous claim, my
maternal grandmother confirmed it. My father was a good
athlete, and on weekends biked, golfed, played tennis, and
coached my brothers' hockey teams. Though he has liberal
political views and a very dry wit (which I am grateful to

have inherited from him), he is not an *unconventional* person. Both parents are the eldest children in families of three, prodigal offspring in a long line of Aryans with youthful appearances, svelte figures, and no major history of illness, medical or psychiatric. (If there had been such a history, I doubt I would have been told anyway.) In a sick and nearly calculated way, I saw them as being the poster couple for WASP repression. It was only as I grew older that I realized that they did nothing out of artifice or fear of judgment; rather, they genuinely *liked* tennis, the country club, summers on the lake, and romantic comedies. *How can they just exist and not even give nod to the* horror *of life?* I thought, fancying myself a mini Mr. Kurtz from *Heart of Darkness,* peering bravely over the edge into the abyss. But there was the rub, looking back on it: they didn't think life was so horrible.

My mother had worked for a large insurance corporation before I was born, and she ended her maternity leave when I was four months old, hiring a nanny to take care of me. My sitter's name was Maureen, and she had been born into an impoverished family in Dublin in the 1930s. She and her thirteen brothers and sisters lived in two rooms on the ground floor of a narrow town house, where they survived on stew and cabbage and warmed their beds with hot irons during the rainy Irish winters. Her parents were raging alcoholics who drifted in and out of their children's lives, though the facts surrounding their absence were never fully explained to me. When her parents left for good, Maureen went to live with her grandmother in an apartment so small that the two were forced to share a bed. During this time Maureen contracted tuberculosis and collapsed in the street. The doctors feared that she would never recover, and her mother, in a rare moment of sobriety, wailed in fear of having a "vegetable for a daughter." Maureen did recover, though, and went to school with a kerchief on her head to hide the bald spots caused by the illness. It was the best time she ever had in school, she told me, because the nuns had never been so kind to her. One night not long after this, Maureen tucked herself in next to her sleeping granny only to wake up beside a cold corpse.

"When you grow up, will you write my biography?" Maureen would frequently ask me. I assured her that I would. I wanted to be an actress and a writer.

"That's a funny combination," people said. But I didn't know why I couldn't be both.

Maureen would weave these little dark fairy tales for me and I would listen, enraptured by the glorious cinematic quality of it all, the romance of corned beef and gangs of grubby street children, envious of her life, the chaos of it. It was a good thing I had her around, because if it were just me, what stories would I possibly have to tell? My family was as sweet and normal as brand-name breakfast cereal. Both sets of my grandparents were still alive. I wasn't allergic to a single thing. I was always being reminded of how lucky I was to be me, how privileged. In the midst of all the placid goodness, I remember feeling that something was missing. Where was the opportunity for conflict? Was this plot even worth a climax? And without that, how could the story ever move forward? How could the character grow?

• • •

IT TOOK ABOUT A YEAR AND A HALF TO BECOME ANOREXIC after I made the decision, in the winter of my eighth-grade year, to try. During this time, I learned about dieting and its more dogmatic echelon, anorexia, about nutrition and calories and ways to get rid of those consumed. I tried *everything,* but still, usually after a day or two of eating very little, I would cave and creep downstairs in the middle of the night and stuff my mouth with whatever was in the cupboards. Nothing could derail my train midbinge—not the children I was babysitting calling out for me, not the knowledge that my family was going out for dinner that night, not the churning of a stomach signifying acute discomfort or the spontaneous and violent reactions of my intestines hours, days, weeks later. Other people's pantries were always more appealing than the food at my house, just like other people's lives seemed inherently more interesting than my own. It was the mystery element, the other-ness of it. There could never be anything exotic about me, or that to which I had ready access. I once ate ten individual-serving bags of my next-door neighbors' Goldfish while dog-sitting for them over a weekend. I tore through the bags like an animal and then walked through my yard back to my house, praying that the family wouldn't notice the theft when they returned.

During this year, I devised strange tests of endurance, or rituals of debasement, the oddest being that I forbade myself to look people directly in the eyes for arbitrary periods of time. I began to attack myself with sharp objects when I was displeased with my performance in eating or in life, which was often. Cutting wasn't something that had come to me out of the blue, either, although I do recall dabbling in self-harm as a youngster. I remember myself at six, standing in front of the mirror in my childhood bedroom, the walls still papered with pink stripes and a trim patterned with bunny rabbits. I had a royal-blue faux-silk scarf I adored for its liquidy feel against my fingers, and I used to wrap it around my neck tightly and watch my reflection go from flesh colored to light blue to purple. I wanted to get the color of my face to match the color of the scarf, but I never succeeded. Much to my chagrin, I was never one of those children who could hold their breath until they fainted when they didn't get their way.

But regardless of this childhood habit, I believed my cutting to also be a derivative behavior. I knew that it was often anorexia's bedfellow, and one of the newer ways in which teen girls were said to express their depressive feelings. It was more gauche than anorexia—a way less impressive feat, the quick swipe of scissors to the forearm—so I valued it less, but I still wanted some way to kill the black mass of *sad* out of me when backed into a corner. I remember seeing the title *A Bright Red Scream* on the shelf in the back of the town library and thinking that I would pick up the habit, just like that. I wanted to scream. This much I knew. But there was no way I could ever *actually* open my throat and let one out. I didn't have the vocabulary, emotional or verbal, to describe how I was feeling, and just considering the possibility of doing so made my muscles freeze and my face go as a blank as a poker player's. What

could I possibly say was wrong? What hardships had I ever
endured?

Whether or not my behavior was imitative, my pain
was very real. I reflect back on the binges and bizarre meth-
ods of self-flagellation with almost more shame and horror
than I do most of my experiences with starvation. And while
I would like to say that I suffered in silence, the reality is
that I was calling out to my friends in ways that even I didn't
understand at the time. Reading in the library, I'd pretend
to drop something and reach to pick it up, hoping that my
friends would notice the tip of a red gash peeking out from
beneath the sleeve of my sweater. I'd often guide conversations toward food—casually, I thought—only to announce
that I had eaten nothing for dinner the night before or
breakfast that morning. Sometimes my admissions would
elicit shrieks of disapproval from my friends, whereas other
times they seemed not to notice, or not to care. I couldn't
blame them; there were real anorexics in my school by then,
so my friends knew I wasn't that bad. Also, I figured they
ought to be horrified by my behavior, as I watched myself
begging to be the center of attention and simultaneously cri-
tiqued myself for it. *They know you're a fraud,* the tiny
voice inside would taunt, its barbs that much more wound-
ing because I knew them to be true.

About eight months into my bingeing and cutting period, a friend told my teacher that my diet consisted mainly
of saltine crackers. My teacher told my mother, who, in
turn, lectured me during a car ride that seemed to last an
eternity. She finished her speech with a nonplussed "We just

never thought we had to worry about you," and it was off to therapy for me. In my evaluation, the doctor, who was the head of a well-reputed eating disorders clinic near my hometown, asked me why I was there.

"Because my friend told my teacher all I eat is crackers."

"Is that true?" she asked.

"I guess so."

But it wasn't. I said nothing about waiting anxiously through *the tick-tick-tick* of the toaster, buttering English muffin after English muffin, scooping peanut butter straight from the jar and inhaling the thick globs straight off the spoon, then chasing it all with a bottle of warm Diet Coke. I didn't say anything about eating pizza slices surreptitiously behind the closed door of my bedroom and then throwing the remaining scraps into the hole underneath my porch to get the last bits out of my reach. (I considered fishing out the dirty crusts occasionally but never did.) Did I withhold the truth because I was ashamed of it, which would be pathologically predictable, or because I wanted so desperately the pure and singular diagnosis of anorexia? Had I been forthright and admitted to all my transgressions, would anorexia, in theory and personal practice, have remained the coveted coup?

"It was dead easy to become anorexic," Naomi Wolf writes in her book *The Beauty Myth*. She's right: it was easy, especially when you had instructions. If you can starve with some consistency, all you need is two weeks under your belt before you begin to eschew food in favor of lining up Hershey's Kisses in your sock drawer, admiring their shiny wrappers as if they were medals of achievement instead of eating them. When Wolf describes her anorexic template, and everyone has one—*that* girl with the baggy clothes and bony extremities who left midway through senior year and returned fleshier and defeated—she chooses to do so poetically. Though Wolf devotes pages to her own anorexia, her template—the anorexic she holds up as the icon of the disease—is Sally, a college classmate. Wolf describes Sally as somewhat of a lovable campus freak, fiercely intelligent but obviously withering underneath her clownish garb. Wolf clearly loves Sally and admires her to a degree—it seems as if she wants to scoop Sally up like a baby and nurse her back to health, but not before absorbing some of Sally's special aura and intellectual veracity. But too soon Sally is gone. Her unclear demise (no elaboration is offered besides the "left suddenly") is a ballet move, a "slow pirouette."

"She'd made it. She had escaped gravity," Wolf writes.

Wolf's one very subtle mistake here is that while the tone might evoke pity, the image is a beautiful, invigorating one. Who doesn't want to fly?

We attempt to debunk the myths of anorexia by couching its intricacies and impurities in pretty language that describes a graceful kind of suffering, a spiritual kind, like that of the fasting girls of the Victorian age who lived off God's will alone. It is a rapturous lingo, a linguistic stone's throw from beatific. When thin, one can dance as Kessa did, as Wolf's template did. Ballerinas, Nadia Comaneci, heroin chic. Faeries. One can wear "faded ginghams and eyelet lace," Sally's outfit of choice, or black tights and no skirt à la Edie Sedgwick. One is a china doll, a shivering Little Match Girl, small and pitiable, so easy to love.

I was in therapy for a year but spent most of each session claiming that I felt better. I was a good liar, and I looked healthy, so what reason did the therapist have to doubt me? But during that time, I never lost my reverence for the pure defiance of anorexia, nor did I stop trying to reach what I thought must be a transcendent state of being. When I went to the clinic for appointments, I watched the bony, exhausted-looking girls exiting the office and felt almost doubled over with envy. *I'll get there. I'll show them.* And after a year and a half of trying, finally one day in the beginning of my sophomore year of high school, my anger at myself reached a new height, the stars aligned, I found my magic combination of foods and crafted a strict exercise regime. As the air chilled outside, I watched with glee as my collarbone emerged from the flesh of my chest, and presto! I was anorexic. But the second I knew I could do it was also the second I knew I could never do it *enough*. Even while hiding out in the frigid upstairs bathroom at my high school during lunch period, counting grapes, or watching the tendons at my elbows jut out when I lifted weights, I still considered myself a completely "fake" anorexic. My diet and exercise knowledge, after all, had come from my seeking it out; I had been through waves of histrionic starvation (punctuated by the aforementioned secret, uncontrollable binges) typical of many teenage girls in the year and a half before I actually began to lose weight. If I were *really* anorexic, I told myself, starving would be *easy*. It would have been a natural inclination, not a skill I had honed. I would be constantly and overwhelmingly convinced of my obesity, not ambivalent with regard to my body image, glimpsing a slender silhouette in a full-length mirror and then viewing a masculine, stocky figure upon second glance. I would go to greater lengths to hide my shrinking figure from people, instead of occasionally wearing tight clothes and delighting in the disgusted or pitying reactions of my friends. I would be adamantly against being treated at all, harbor no covert desire to be spoon-fed or locked up, "saved from myself," as so many pop singers crooned. I would be this and this, instead of that. Loopholes. The conclusion of all this was Not Sick, and if the girls in the books or featured on the afternoon talk shows said that they sometimes felt inadequate, well, that was because that was a *symptom* of their very real eating disorders, whereas my self-deprecation, I was sure, was based on sound evidence. How could anyone prove otherwise?

CHAPTER 4

IDOL WORSHIP

AFTER THREE MONTHS OF SERIOUSLY RESTRICTING, I WAS
admitted as an outpatient to an eating disorders program at
Silver Hill Hospital, a general mental health facility located
in the town directly north of mine. I was fifteen years old. I
had been in therapy and nutritional counseling before and had
joined a small therapy group that met at my school, but I was,
for all intents and purposes (despite my acquired knowledge
of the subject), clueless about what to expect. On a Monday
during my Christmas vacation, my dad took me to the hospital for my evaluation. We drove through the woodsy enclave
of northern New Canaan and pulled into a long circular
driveway that led to a white colonial mansion perched atop
a hill. If there hadn't been a sign out front, you might have
mistaken it for any of the other large houses set far back
from the road and hidden behind tall, handsome elms.

The evaluation took place in one of a small cluster of buildings next to the main house. I sat in a stiff armchair staring at framed paintings of ducks floating on ponds and other New England scenes on the walls until a social worker called my name. When I was in his dark office, he asked me the litany of questions I would become very familiar with over the coming years: *What is your name? What is the date? Who is the president of the United States? Do you ever feel like hurting yourself or others?* After I answered the questions, he asked me awkwardly if he could see my "body image." I felt ashamed—was he implying that I wasn't thin enough to be admitted? Or maybe my face, naturally round and babyish, led him to believe the rest of my body was also soft and fleshy? I unzipped my red North Fleece and pulled it back to reveal my torso, sheathed in my favorite baby-blue shirt with three-quarter-length sleeves and a wide neck.

"Okay," he said softly. "Okay."

The social worker told my father that I would start the program the next day. I could be dropped off at noon, in time for lunch, and picked up after post-dinner therapy group at 6:45. In between, I'd participate in an adolescent group, have a snack, then attend two eating disorders groups and have individual meetings with my doctor and my therapist. I'd be on my own for breakfast.

When I arrived the next day, my social worker ushered me from the doctor's office to a small annex of the main-house dining room where the eating-disordered, or EDO, patients ate. Two staff members and two patients sat waiting for lunch to arrive. The patients were introduced as Kristin and Jamie. Jamie had tiny dark ringlets and a pallid, chubby face that almost touched the place mat, she was so hunched over. She looked about my age. Kristin looked younger. She could have been a normal preteen, but I noticed hints of wrongness: the straw-dead ends of her mousy-brown hair, the deep lavender circles beneath her wide, panicked eyes. I said hello meekly and sat down.

I heard the kitchen door swing open and saw a tiny old cafeteria lady shuffle across the room and heard *clack* as my tray was placed on the table in front of me. I had always assumed that when I was forced to eat, the carnal person inside me would be immediately resuscitated, and I would lose forever the tenuous hold I had over my appetite. I glanced warily at the tray. Chicken, rice, grapes, milk. Whole? Skim? I took a deep breath. Was the anxiety real or was I fabricating it? *Maybe if there weren't so much food. Maybe if it were something different, not rice, all those tiny little grains, all that divisibility. Maybe if it were an apple instead of grapes. Countable. Mass of chicken. If you make it small, it will be manageable. You can't look like you're enjoying it. That would be humiliating. Maybe just take it slow. At dinner tonight, tomorrow, the next day: that's when you can begin to eat normally. You'll just make the decision, and so it will be. For now, though, you'll approach with caution.*

I tapped the chicken with the fork, half expecting it to move. When was the last time I had eaten meat? I couldn't recall. I hadn't indulged in cooked food for months. Once I chewed and swallowed the warm grilled breast, felt the protein course through my body, I would realize how much I had missed it, and I'd never be able to give it up again.

I painstakingly sliced and arranged and declared a new rule for each sliver of food. *Bite this in half.* To live with anorexia is to live in a fascist state of being, one ruled by a cruel and illogical board of Kafkaesque tyrants. They squabble among one another incessantly but usually can come to an agreement when the subject is food and whether to eat it and if so, how. A rule inexplicably coalesces from nothingness and turns into gospel in a matter of milliseconds. You are demonized for not knowing it should have been mandated months ago. Awareness of the idiosyncrasies of another's anorexia only leads to further rule-making. *Well, Susie taps the table three times before she takes a sip. Now you have to do it* four *times.*

And I suppose this is what it must have been like for Kristin during this meal, watching me treat my food like a spreadsheet, curl my lips away to avoid touching the fork, like Kessa of *The Best Little Girl in the World.* "The food on her lips would make her unclean," Levenkron wrote. It felt instinctual, this retreat from the meat, but it wasn't an original move, couldn't be copyrighted. I wasn't thinking about authenticity right in that moment, though. I was thinking about the chicken, the fork, and Kristin. She was watching me with the lack of subtlety typical of the prepubescent and aped my movements. I broke my intense concentration every few minutes to mentally note her adherence to my model. I let it happen. It made me feel good. Powerful, maybe.

These nutritional tics were the only things I had over Kristin or anyone there, I would soon come to believe. During my first group session I scanned the room and pronounced quietly in my head: *Thinner, thinner, thinner. Her knuckles could cut glass.* Most of them had been inpatient already and were still waifs, and they spoke nonchalantly of the other places they had been hospitalized, the lessons they had learned there, as if they were talking about school or summer camp. In the patient hierarchy, I may as well have been a kindergartener to their master's degrees. They were at home in this world, sitting Indian-style on the floor, flopping down onto the big leather couches, and I, again, was outside it all. I was not sick enough to be there. I shook my leg vigorously in a feeble attempt to burn off snack calories. Their bodies represented their determination, while mine revealed my weakness; their pursed lips and terse answers spoke of their adherence to anorexic credo, my moralizing and openness of spirit attested to my lack of dedication, my falsehood. Kristin burned a hole in my ankle with her stare and flailed her leg faster.

I hesitate to be even this specific. Details are venomous to this work. Will someone on a unit read this and start to shake his or her legs? I learned this trick from a book, though I no longer remember which one. If I hadn't read it somewhere, I would have quickly learned it from my fellow patients, who often had to be told to stop bouncing their feet under a table rocking like a rowboat on a choppy sea. None of my habits belonged to me. I was Oscar Wilde's "most people," and ashamed of it.

Kristin hovered near me for the few weeks I was an outpatient. She pulled me into the living room during a break. Among the dated earth-toned furniture, she asked me what I weighed. Had I reached target? Critical?

"In the hospital I was in before here, I had a feeding tube," she said. In later iterations of the story she added "a machine that helped me breathe." She cited her lowest weight frequently, which was never the same, and giggled when I noticed the bevy of instructions next to her name on the dry erase board on the adolescent unit: dayroom observation, no napkins, must be weighed backward, locked bathroom.

"When I first got here I would exercise in my room and throw up and hide food in my napkin." She seemed amused; a tiny smirk was visible in her bluish lips. I didn't wonder why, because I believed that if I were that sick, I would be proud of myself, too.

So why was she so interested in me? I assumed because I was a treatment neophyte and she could easily awe me with her history. That flicker of "impressive" across my face was probably enough to allow her a few moments of peace, as her adoption of my every food ritual allowed me. Thus we became trapped in this miniature folie à deux, relying on each other to validate our illnesses. We conspired to hide food, first slipping crumbs beneath the table, later audaciously ripping chunks out of muffins and tossing them into the garbage when the staff wasn't looking. We'd glance at each other and smile. Gloriously guilty by association. *We are smarter / more intense / sneakier / more / more / more than everyone else.*

I must have known that in some way Kristin found me a viable source of competition. This was years before a friend and I determined that anorexics, like members of the Mafia, tend to keep their friends close and their enemies closer, but in some way I must have sensed that Kristin's interest in me was rooted in the fact that she found me threatening. She didn't cling to Jamie. She rejoiced in debunking the myths Jamie told about her illness behind Jamie's back.

"She always says that she was so skinny when she first came here, and that she eats so fast in order to get it over with. I don't think that's true."

I agreed, as usual. I needed to, otherwise I would risk damaging our relationship and my security in my sickness, something that I hadn't had before and wanted to hold on to.

Like a good novitiate, Kristin studied and meditated on the subject of anorexia. She always carried books about anorexia checked out from the hospital's library. In group one evening, Sam, a teenage girl with a sideways smile and frizzy red hair, spoke with a near-graduate's certainty on the perils of reading books about eating disorders.

"You can trick yourself into thinking you're doing something good, but they can be really bad for you," Sam said. "Especially *that* one." She pointed across the room to where *Wasted* sat on a coffee table beside Kristin, who grinned with a sheepish pride at being singled out as the transgressor, the *worst*.

The therapist concurred with Sam, and then added a personal spin on the subject. "Marya Hornbacher is my daughter's best friend. She's been hospitalized since this book came out. She should not be held up as a model for recovery in any sense."

I felt cheated when I heard this. How could you write about sickness and recovery if you didn't actually recover?

But then again, I reasoned, could I blame her? Who really wanted a role model for recovery, anyway? What was the point of having a goal like "be normal"?

After three weeks, I had succeeded only in losing more weight. The powers that be determined I was to be admitted as an inpatient. My hospital doctor made me sign a paper indicating that I was committing myself even though I was only fifteen.

"Didn't I tell you if you dropped below that weight I would see you on Main Three?" he asked pompously. I nodded, but no, he hadn't said that. He was mistaking me for another of his patients. I worried for a moment that it was a bad sign for me, the fact that he couldn't remember who I was.

That day, as I knelt down to tie my shoes after being weighed, I told Kristin my magical number. My smirk was obvious. Less than an hour later, I found her crouching by a table in the hallway, despondent over the fact that another patient ("My name is Kylie, and I am here for depression and self-mutilation") had told her that she looked "healthy," which is a terrible insult to the anorexic. Whole group therapy sessions are devoted to anticipating friends telling you that you look "healthy" when you return home after treatment. I knelt beside Kristin as she wept furiously.

"You're so much thinner than I am," she cried. "You're so much cuter and thinner than I am. Everyone's going to like you better."

"I'm not, I'm not, I swear I'm not," I said, on the one hand baffled by her feelings, on the other enormously flattered. The twenty-four hours before my admission went much like that. Kristin would collapse from professed inadequacy, I would comfort her, she would recover momentarily, and the cycle, immensely satisfying to both of us, would begin again.

That night, instead of going home, I was escorted up to Main 3, one tiny hall on the third floor with many locked doors and no keys. As I settled into my room that evening, Kristin slunk into the doorway and asked to try on a pair of my pants.

"I don't have any clothes here. My mom keeps saying she'll bring them."

My roommate, Liz, was watching the interaction. Liz was my age but tall and lanky, with feline eyes and a deep monotone voice. When we had met earlier that day, after her admission, she was wearing a black turtleneck, and it made her look like her head was an apple wobbling on a toothpick. In group, she would cop to being bulimic and depressed, but she refused to say she was anorexic. That evening, we shared our stats: we were the exact same number of pounds below the "critical" weight, but I decided that she was still "better" than I was, mainly because she was taller, which made her look leaner. Plus, Liz had been an athlete and said she couldn't stay cooped up in our room without burning off some calories, so she got up at night and jogged a little back and forth. I followed suit, mostly to save face—I loathed exercise, even though I had kept to my routine until right before I was admitted, when I abandoned it altogether because I was too tired to make it through. The fact that her compulsion seemed genuine whereas I knew mine to be a farce gave her, naturally, more cred.

Liz eyed Kristin suspiciously and told me later that she had silently pleaded with me in her mind, *Don't do it.* She hadn't been in treatment before, either, but like me, she knew what was going on. It wasn't about needing an outfit.

Kristin and I snuck into Kristin's room and switched trousers. I caught a glimpse of her relatively sturdy thighs from behind and gloated imperceptibly. I was learning to love this attention, this Pyrrhic victory. Later that evening, I went into the dayroom to watch television wearing flannel pajama shorts. Kristin came out in sweatpants and then retreated to her room to change into shorts. When she sat next to me, she circled her thigh with her hands and stared at mine. I lifted my feet off the floor to make the gap between my legs seem larger. Had I been older, less enamored of the straightforward compare-contrast system anorexia offered, I would have said something, I would have told her she was being ridiculous. Maybe I would have changed into pants myself.

Over the next month, things changed. Liz's insurance ran out, and she went home. I was left alone in the room with nothing but a memoir I had checked out of the facility's library about a male anorexic who ran away from home and checked himself into motels when he felt like starving without being bothered. He died in one of those motel rooms. I tucked his story into the back of my brain, adding it to the scale against which my illness was measured.

You ought to just cut your ties with everyone and get the job done with. He *did it. He was so much* better *than you are.*

And of course I gained weight. Every morning I stood in front of the tiny bathroom mirror and swung my arms in wide circles like a swimmer preparing to do laps, noting with dismay the decreasing visibility of each and every rib. I mourned my ghostly former figure, which I saw as slight only in hindsight. Another girl was admitted, a girl my age named Lisa. She had previously been at Cornell, that legendary behemoth of hospitals in a nearby county, and she was *really* thin. Kristin marveled at her tiny wrists, but Lisa recoiled at Kristin's clumsiness. I was more discreet. I asked Lisa about her previous hospitalization, the girls there, their statistics, tried to get a clear enough picture so I could compare myself to them, so I would know where I ranked. She told me of the anorexic twins, a girl who binged on water in the shower, another who ran away shrieking when they gave her soup even though she'd been inpatient for six months.

"Was there someone on the unit that was considered the 'best' anorexic?" I asked her.

"I guess Juliette," she replied, unenthusiastically.

I thought about this Juliette girl with envy. I didn't know her or what she looked like. Blond? Tall? Friendly? A nibbler, or a cut-into-small-pieces girl? I envisioned her as

pretty and young, a testament to my still-naive, glossy view
of the disease. I wanted to know what it was like to be her. I
imagined her as satisfied with her anorexia. Princess of the
skeletons. If only I could be so secure in it. Then I could let go.

• • •

THE THERAPY GROUPS FOR ADOLESCENTS WERE HELD IN THE
cold white basement after lunch every weekday. This was
when all the inpatients on Main 3 and the outpatient kids
from the surrounding suburban areas who came to the hospital instead of going to school would gather with a therapist. On Wednesdays, the group was led by Dan Holloway,
a bearded middle-aged man with a stuffy, old-fashioned
aura and a voice as numbing as Vicodin. In his group, we
would tell stories. Our stories. Every week, one person
would get the chance to regale the group with all the details
of his or her fall from childish grace. A whole forty-five minutes all to one's self. Everyone enjoyed hearing the troubles
of others, the triumphs and heartaches and blowouts fit
for after-school specials. A girl told us about her overdose,
acknowledged the possibility that she had swallowed pills
to endear herself to her beloved high school chemistry
teacher, who also had depression. Another said she knew
there was a problem when she was high on ecstasy, lazily
dragging a butcher knife up her arm in a room full of people
who, even high out of their minds, gawked at her in horror.
A girl with dark hair and droopy eyes and a diagnosis of
"psychotic depression" said that a man who was not really
there had chased her around her house with a knife. An
obese girl named Tia with a poorly bandaged self-inflicted

wound on her forearm said she had been afraid of the toilet ever since her grandmother told her that a snake would emerge from the drain and bite her on the butt when she sat down. After she revealed this phobia, Tia joined us in giggling.

The day I was to tell my story, I anticipated the reactions of the other kids, their soft, pitying looks or swift, shocked inhales. I wondered if this time, in this place as quiet as a rectory and cold as a catacomb, I would be able to condense the rambling yarn, skip the flubbed lines, the missed cues, expand on the really dramatic scenes. I wondered if I could fulfill my need, and that of my audience, for the triumvirate of storytelling: beauty, regularity, and form.

When I opened my mouth to speak, the most wonderfully cohesive personal narrative poured forth. It was similar to the kind I had often read in magazine articles, ones that began with a diet gone awry. There was no desire in my story, no plan; I had never wanted to be sick, nor had I paraded around school declaring I was faint or made friends online and asked them to help me starve. I had grasped control, and then the control had grasped me. The thread unspooled itself into uncomplicated anorexia, and the conclusion was poor little me, stuck in the hospital. As I told it, I was hoping with all I had in me—in vain, I knew—that it was the truth, and that the truth, indeed, would set me free.

• • •

MY FIRST INCLINATION, BEFORE RECRACKING THE COVER OF *Wasted: A Memoir of Anorexia and Bulimia,* is to quote

Homer's verse about Odysseus, the warrior whom destiny
had forced to travel through hostile and bizarre environs.

> Sing to me of the man, Muse, the man of twists and turns
> driven time and again off course . . .

Or, better yet, Virgil's *Aeneid*:

> Wars and a man I sing—an exile driven on by fate
> he was the first to flee the coast of Troy,
> destined to reach Lavinian shores and Italian soil
> yet many blows he took on land and sea from the gods above—
> thanks to cruel Juno's relentless rage—and many losses
> he bore in battle too, before he could find a city
> bring his gods to Latium, source of the Latin race,
> the Alban lords and the high walls of Rome
> Tell me, Muse, how it all began.

After all, if there really were a canon of eating disorders literature, *Wasted* would surely be a cornerstone, a
beloved, poetic contemporary classic. To illustrate just how
influential it has been to my generation of anorexics, allow
me to share a recent anecdote from a friend's engagement
party, where I bumped into a college classmate of mine. The
girl was a few years my junior who, I knew from our late-
night drunken confessions of sins past, had been hospitalized twice for anorexia during her early-teenage years.
Wondering what her thoughts might be now on the subject
of anorexia, literature, and "awareness," I asked her if she

had ever read *Wasted*. I couldn't get the question out of my mouth before she answered, "Of course!"

If *Wasted* is the epic that fed the wanderlust of so many young women, Marya Hornbacher, then, would be the Virgil of the poem, guiding us into the Inferno, singing the song of her muse, O Anorexia.

I have not touched *Wasted* since soon after I bought it from that bookstore in 1998. The copy I have is a new one, purchased off Amazon in 2009, from the seventh printing with a new afterword that contains a reading guide and an update on Hornbacher's life. It still ends up heavily underlined and dog-eared. We know that Marya Hornbacher was a good anorexic, so good, in fact, that her whole life was essentially co-opted by the pro-ana movement. Hornbacher's book offered mesmerized adolescents, myself included, step-by-step instructions for how to lose weight the dramatic way. Eat this, not that. Follow my lead, kids, and you can be as good as (if not "better than") me. This was, of course, not what she said in her writings, but it was what some young ones heard. Hornbacher imagined dieting, and later anorexia, with all its romantic Victorian "fasting girl" connotations, as a route to Specialness, "like hopscotch."

When I first read the book, I latched on to any and all eating-disordered-related materials (thinspiration, though the term had not been coined yet; those of us on the frontlines of the pro-ana movement used examples packaged as "awareness" or "education" or "acceptance," meant to counteract the dreaded "denial" or "secrecy" or "tact"). I read just about every book on the subject, sometimes more than once. I browsed awareness websites, frequented chat rooms, and read personal web pages detailing individual horror stories—stories like the one I envisioned for myself. I even had a family friend, who worked for ABC News, get me the videos of the infamous *20/20* episodes featuring Peggy Claude-Pierre from the channel's archives. At the time, Claude-Pierre was seen as an angelic rogue therapist willing to treat the most difficult of cases in a program she established called the Montreux Clinic. I salivated over footage of Claude-Pierre carrying skeletal patients down the stairs of the gorgeous Victorian mansion in British Columbia where she housed her practice, spoon-feeding them bananas and yogurt, stroking their hair and whispering encouragement. I wanted to be small enough that she would scoop me up in a gentle bear hug, sick enough for someone to love me back to health. I even found the phone number for the center and called it a number of times, each time getting a recorded message, each time hanging up, unable to think of what I would say if a real human ever answered. (Montreux was shut down by the Canadian government in 1999 for a number of health code violations, including holding patients against their will. When I heard about the court case against them, I commiserated with an online pal, an anorexic teenager from Victoria who admitted to biking by the facility on a weekly basis.)

Since my first hospitalization in 2000, however, I have moved steadily away from seeking out such "triggering" materials; indeed, I began to regard them almost as kryptonite. If I was watching television and it was announced that Dr. Phil would have anorexics on his show that day, I would pounce on the remote and change the channel. If anorexia or eating disorders came up in conversation, I would silently and nonchalantly exit the room. In later hospitalizations, if girls began to talk about weight, I would hum low to myself so I couldn't decipher the specifics. Sometimes I was bold enough to ask them to change the topic, which was kind of code for "I'm out of the game." I was fanatical about it at times, but I don't regret this. I think it was rather smart, in hindsight. After all, if you have lung cancer, why would you sit near someone who is smoking?

In the past few years, I've finally developed a skin when it comes to the disease, and I don't need to avoid these triggers so vigilantly. It doesn't throw me into a tailspin of self-evaluation when I hear of someone who was hospitalized once more than I was, or a girl I knew from a treatment center back in the day being readmitted. Diet articles don't have me frantically structuring a life-and-eating-plan, nor does even the threat of a close friend's relapse sway my faith in my own preference for health. The reasons for this, paradoxically, are that (a) at one point I got worse, and after so many go-arounds, I was able to see anorexia as the most insidious and hateful of all things, not an art to be perfected or a calling to be answered. And then (b) I got better.

My distrust of Marya Hornbacher and her book is a subject on which I have ruminated for almost a decade with little time spent actually examining the material. I pushed thoughts of her writing to the side and instead focused on the myriad young women I met in hospitals with underlined, worn copies and diet plans directly lifted from the pages. I've raged about how a recovering anorexic, one with still-fresh memories of the scorpion-battle competition of hospital wards and not a small amount of awareness about the Nature, capital N, of eating disorders, could publish something so blatantly didactic. About this point, I remain firmly disapproving. Hornbacher herself cops to having been inspired at nine years old by Kessa Dietrich of *The Best Little Girl in the World,* whom she reverently describes as "withdrawn, reserved, cold, wholly absorbed in her own obsession, perfectly pure . . . I decided [after reading it] that if I did nothing else with my life, I would be an anorexic when I grew up." She had to have anticipated, given her own experience, that perhaps some young girl would take from her story what she took from Levenkron's book.

"I was on vacation with my family so I couldn't do anything, but I took notes," my roommate Liz told me when we first met of her experience with *Wasted.*

How smart, I thought.

Reflecting on that comment years later, Liz wrote to me in an e-mail, "My reaction to the book was that I wanted to do what she did . . . I still didn't think I was sick [when I was admitted to the hospital] so I strove to become sick. I knew I was depressed, but no amount of convincing would lead me to believe I was anorexic. She gave me something to strive for."

I've let my messy feelings about *Wasted* stew inside me as I've grown older and been educated. My disapproval has gained a pretty prose. I expected, therefore, to be filled with rage from page one when I reread it. My fists were up when I opened to the introduction, "Notes on the Netherworld." The thirteen-year-old in my mind still perceived Hornbacher's tone as mocking, rife with a confidence I would surely, and justifiably, never possess. "I am the *best* anorexic ever," she says, sticking her tongue out. "The rest of you are the peons to my anorexic royalty!" And yet as I began to read anew, I was filled with something other than hatred: liberation, because the urge to compare myself to her was such a small twinge of feeling it was barely perceptible; frustration, too, for a number of reasons; also a deep sympathy; and awe, even, because she is a fantastic writer.

As I continued to read, I begrudgingly acknowledged similarities between myself and Hornbacher on levels both superficial and eerie. Shallow, explicable types include: a preoccupation with self-construction/"personae," an affinity for books and quotations, a "love affair with hotels, which has yet to end," a preference to communicate with my mother via e-mail. I wondered if one could chalk these things up to having an artist's/writer's "soul." The creepier sense arose when I recognized parts of my own writing in hers. Little things, at first: sentence structure, the slip-and-slide of phrasing, capitalization of words to emphasize their Objectivity, things that an untrained eye, or perhaps a less paranoid one, would never notice at all. *A New Me,* she writes (personae). *Nature,* I say, *capital N.*

There were larger coincidences, too. My early attempt at straight memoir, which began as purely stream-of-consciousness journaling less than a year after my third hospitalization in

2003 and then curdled at people's suggestions of "Hey, you should write a book!" contains passages that are embarrassingly similar to Hornbacher's. When I started to feel the tug of the uncanny, I went on a scavenger hunt for my old material, long since banished to an external hard drive, to examine the similarities, both linguistic and experiential. What I found left me questioning a great many things about my experience, Hornbacher's, and that of a normal child growing up in a baffling, modern world.

First off, Hornbacher:

I was about four when I first fell into the mirror. I sat in front of my mother's bathroom mirror singing and playing dress up by myself, digging through my mother's huge magical box of stage makeup that sighed a musty perfumed breath when you opened its brass latch. I painted my face with elaborate greens and blues on the eyes, bright streaks of red on the cheeks, garish orange lipstick, then I stared at myself in the mirror for a long time. I suddenly felt a split in my brain: I didn't recognize her. I divided into two: the self in my head and the girl in the mirror. It was a strange, not unpleasant feeling of disorientation. I began to return to the mirror often, to see if I could get that feeling back. If I sat very still and thought: Not me–not me–not me over and over, I could retrieve the feeling of being two girls, staring at each other through the glass of the mirror.

I didn't know then that I would eventually have that feeling all the time. Ego and image. Body and brain. The "mirror phase" of child development took on new meaning for me. "Mirror phase" essentially describes my life.

And mine, unedited:

A lot of contemplation about stars and waking hours led me to the front of my mirror one day. This little-girl body, this "Kelsey" and her life wasn't necessarily real; the inner monologue of her psyche was the only thing that could possibly wrench her from a half-true existence, living in this world of empty explanations designed to make people feel better, where bodies encased minds and no one seemed to care what went on in there. I stared myself down. I looked into my big brown eyes while simultaneously convincing myself of the lack of connection between the image in the mirror and the ME in my head. Who is that girl? You don't know her. You don't. Separate. And for one split second I felt my brain pull a fraction of a hair away from my body. For that one second I legitimately felt like I didn't know her, the girl in the mirror. And I swear, it was a physical sensation, like the crack of a small bone.

For years I thought of that moment with a mixture of fear and awe, imagining that I had somehow reached a plane of knowledge that most other people, or people my age, perhaps, never got to. The fear part was associated with the physical sensation, which I found to be extremely disconcerting and shrank from thinking about, replacing it with the thoughts of myself as a deep soul, a baby philosopher.

It was over a decade before I learned about the French psychoanalyst Lacan and his theories. At first I believed I had found proof that my reaction to my image in the mirror was, in fact, not a unique incident that marked me as a hyper-conscious human being but rather a cornerstone of

Western psychoanalytic theory. One of Lacan's major stages of development he coined the "mirror stage," which he considered a crucial part of the life of an infant. The infant sees its image in the mirror and connects the image with its own self in order to alleviate the "aggressive tension between the subject and the image." Later, the infant begins to believe in the mastery of its body when he/she watches him/herself rise into the upright position, thereby solidifying the infant's belief that he/she is in control of his/her corporeal form. The body ceases to appear "in bits and pieces" and becomes intrinsically connected to the brain; human beings, therefore, NEED an image of themselves in order to have an intact ego and a sense of stability in themselves and the universe at large.

The above paragraph details what I learned about the mirror stage recently and largely illuminates points that make it quite different from what I experienced as a child. Despite the fact that I must have learned in my early infancy that I was master of my form by watching myself in the mirror and connecting my movements with the distinct orders in my brain that came before them, I did not ever seem to rid myself of that "aggressive tension." Perhaps (and I am obviously grasping in the dark here) my ego was formed in that part of my babyhood when I watched myself rise on wobbly legs and then subsequently shattered when I forced my brain to disconnect from my body. I seemed to understand, preternaturally, that mirrors lie: the images are always different and are so incongruous with the way we feel inside. It's as if I spent a majority of my life looking in the mirror at a stranger. "Why, she doesn't look anything like me!"

I've tried for years now to heal that wound born from

conscious alienation, the one that no doubt made it easier for
me to think about, and thus treat, my body as a foreign object.

Obviously Hornbacher says it a hell of a lot more succinctly than I do, but the meat of it is the same: small child has strange moment when she disassociates from her own image. This wasn't the thing that really shook my foundation, though. As I glided through Hornbacher's childhood, giggling intermittently when I thought of what a cute little imp she must have been, I stopped dead midsentence.

"I dropped to my knees, pressing my nails into the palms of my hands—"

And that was it, right there, because this was a habit I have that I had often used to assure myself of my inherently masochistic spirit (read: the inevitability of its manifestation, anorexia, and my lack of complicity). You see, I have two rather large calluses smack in the middle of both palms from digging my middle fingernail into the skin there for, oh, as long as I can remember.

"Like Jesus," people always said.

"Christ was the first anorexic," asserts the narrator of *The Passion of Alice,* which I read at summer camp when I was fourteen. "Most people don't realize, but it's true."

"I mean, it's really more about lesbianism," my bunkmate said, scrunching up her face in disapproval. She knew the psychology section of her local library, too. Her older sister, a slight, freckly redhead, had attended the camp until she started instead attending hospital programs. "One doctor at Renfrew said she was the worst anorexic he'd ever seen." As my bunkmate said this, she beamed with by-proxy pride.

The last time I was hospitalized, in 2004, a friendly Mrs. Claus–plump nurse noticed my pseudo-stigmata and said, "Oh, dear!" She had me cover them with Band-Aids, which I loved because it just succeeded in drawing attention to the presence of something-beneath. I hadn't known it was a strange habit until one day during my sophomore year of high school, when a boy who was flirting with me was stroking my hands.

"What *is* that?"

I was bemused by his shock, and responded, "I had no idea it was weird."

Or did I? Was it possible that I had actually developed this habit *after* I read *Wasted* and, desperate to amend my history to include the seeds of illness, wove it into the narrative of my life so meticulously that now, at this age, I cannot determine what is real and what I have "consciously" (term used loosely) created? Are the quirks of language I once thought instinctive just an imitation of Hornbacher's style? Did the incident in front of the mirror, which I think I remember as traumatizing, really happen at all? And, to further this idea, were Hornbacher's life and book written and edited in a similar way, she having been attracted to Levenkron's Kessa, to the icons of the tortured female she quotes so often in her own text? Sylvia Plath, Anne Sexton, Lewis Carroll's plucky, darling Alice? Poor drowned Ophelia?

CHAPTER 5

THE ANOREXIA SPECTRUM

ONCE, WHEN I WAS IN COLLEGE, MY FRIEND MICHAEL TOLD me about how at his high school they used to differentiate between the girls who pretended to be or relished being anorexic and those who appeared to suffer more. "We used to say that Andrea Menken was a *real* anorexic." At the time, I squirmed in my chair, traced the edge of my glass with my finger. I was on the serious road to health at this point—though there was one relapse left in my future, unbeknownst to me then—but I still felt waves of shame emanating from me. How pathetic would he think I was if he knew that even at my sickest I hadn't been a "real" anorexic? How manipulative was I not to tell him at that very moment? *You ought to just out yourself immediately as a fraud. You're a liar simply by remaining silent.* Not that anyone ever took me seriously when I tried to explain that

I was a "fake" anorexic. I understood why they wouldn't acquiesce to me on that point, but I also knew, deep inside, that because of its origins, I could never really believe in the validity of my own illness.

It was surprising to me to hear that "normal" people, laypeople, believed in a distinction between the real and the fake, too. I thought that was a talent, or perhaps a delusion, of discernment that came specifically from one too many holidays on the psych ward and a serious personal investment in the idea of anorexia as craft, skill, or competitive endeavor, complete with minor and major leagues. But maybe the real anorexic is a character that everyone knows, and her authenticity is palpable for all. This character is one that I've been searching for in vain for years now, both the actualized emaciated girl inside of me and the one out there in the collective unconscious. Who is she, and what makes her more authentic than her counterparts? What is it about her that we want so much to know and sometimes to possess?

The first place I go to look for her is, of course, the clinical definition. Over the course of editing this book, the fifth edition of the Diagnostic and Statistics Manual, or *DSM-V*, came out, debuting a much wider definition of anorexia nervosa than its precursor, the *DSM-IV*. (This is presumably to make treatment more widely available.) The bible of psychiatry, current edition, characterizes anorexia as:

    A. Restriction of energy intake relative to requirements, leading to a significantly low body weight in the context of age, sex, developmental trajectory, and physical health. *Significantly low weight* is defined as a weight that is less than minimally normal or, for children and adolescents, less than that minimally expected.

B. Intense fear of gaining weight or of becoming fat, or persistent behavior that interferes with weight gain, even though at a significantly low weight.

C. Disturbance in the way in which one's body weight or shape is experienced, undue influence of body weight or shape on self-evaluation, or persistent lack of recognition of the seriousness of the current low body weight.

The weight requirement—vague as it is—is usually all but brushed aside by the powers that be, as it's not the most reliable barometer of acuteness. In fact, the *DSM-V*, which was released in May of 2013, has a far less stringent weight requirement than the *DSM-IV* did, which shows that the medical community is becoming less insistent upon that component of the illness. This is a step in the right direction, given the numerous problems that result from resting the definition of anorexia on weight. Let's say, for example, that when someone begins restricting, he or she is overweight, and now, after a period of severe dieting, he or she is at a healthy weight. The body of this sufferer could easily be in worse medical condition than, say, that of someone who is maintaining at 70 percent of their healthy weight. Also, after starving for a protracted period of time (or very seriously for a short time) the metabolism slows to adjust to the body's level of intake. A person in that position might be ingesting far fewer calories than he or she should to maintain a normal weight and yet still, there it is, the "normal" shape. The body is a strange, sometimes arbitrarily resilient vessel and it can withstand horrors one wouldn't imagine possible. Women have been known to maintain periods until they reach drastically low weights, their bodies going through the motions as if they were capable of carrying babies. (Amenorrhea, or absence of a menstrual cycle, was also a diagnostic requirement in the *DSM-IV*, and has been removed because there were simply too many exceptions to the rule.)

"Anorexics don't always look too thin," my friend Jackie, who is recovering, says. "They just look *wrong*."

So A is iffy. It is, of course, indicative of a problem, but the *authenticity* of an eating disorder is not contingent upon it.

B and C, these are trickier. These symptoms (minus the "persistent lack of recognition of the seriousness of the current low body weight") are probably present in a vast majority of adolescent girls, and quite a few women, too. Conversely, there are also anorexics that, ironically enough, don't care (or claim not to care) very much about their size. I once knew a bulimic who said her illness was more about the self-inflicted pain of purging than any concern over whether she was fat. For another person, this behavior might be classified as "persistent behavior that interferes with weight gain," but this young woman was at normal weight. (Binging and purging doesn't always lead to weight loss, though it has horrific ramifications on the body, many more immediate and severe than those caused by persistent starvation.) Kate Taylor, the editor of the 2008 book *Going*

Hungry: Writers on Desire, Self-Denial, and Overcoming Anorexia, claims that she didn't think too much about her weight during dire times. "I believed . . . that my weight loss was the result of a series of rational acts, which had nothing to do with being thin," she writes. And later, "While I was anorexic, I believed that I saw myself accurately and that I knew I was too thin. I could see my bony wrists and the sad way that my jeans sagged where my butt should have been."

I understand this. When I was a fledgling anorexic, I was attached to the idea that I was fat and that I needed to get thin. At first it felt a little like playacting: I was forcing myself to worry about my weight because I thought that was what I was supposed to do, and because that was what would make me feel motivated to eat less, which was more important to me than losing weight. It was an age-appropriate activity, and it made me feel like I was finally joining the ranks of my female peers. Intellectually, I knew I was thin, but I just wanted to lose weight, to be thinner, to be thin *enough.* When I relapsed in my early twenties, I experienced a disembodied aversion to my appearance similar to Kate Taylor's. I saw myself as too thin, was acutely embarrassed by my appearance and whatever attention it attracted, but by then I was too dependent upon the process of the illness, the rituals and the secrecy and all that, to give it up. I would frequently tell my doctor that if I could have a feeding tube, I would take it. I didn't care if I had to gain weight, as long as I didn't have to actually eat.

But that might have been big talk.

So that disturbance of bodily appearance can't be the

be-all and end-all of anorexia. None of the clinical symptoms are the crux of "real" anorexia, but that isn't surprising. Rarely does a diagnosis succeed in encapsulating all the idiosyncrasies of an illness, especially a psychiatric one. How can such clinical, dry language describe the horrifying and all-encompassing hallucinations of a schizophrenic or the wild, Technicolor joy of a bout of mania?

So I move to the other books—memoirs, novels, doctors' accounts—because I think the poetry of the disorder will give me insight. I approach the books with a good deal of trepidation. I am still terrified that poring over the clinical reports and personal accounts will eventually, if not immediately, inspire me to stay up until all hours contemplating, calculating:

> *If Anorexic A was this tall and weighed this much, then she was definitely more underweight than I was, which means I wasn't a good enough anorexic. Anorexic B was my height and my weight, but she was in the hospital more times than I was, so she was a better anorexic than I was, too. Anorexic C was never in the hospital nor was she ever technically underweight, but she is still better than I am. I don't know why, but she is.*

That's always the word, too. *Better.* Meaning, in a frightening reversal of valuation, "sicker." Rarely, if ever, am I allowed to label myself "better" than another. The result of settling on my inferiority? *Why not make another go of it? Finish what you started. Maybe when you weigh what the narrator of this article did, you'll feel like a real contender.*

"Then I went on the Internet for a checklist of what symptoms occur when you're anorexic or bulimic, and I went through them to make sure I had every single one so I could try to be the perfect anorexic," Brittany, a Renfrew Center patient, told photographer Lauren Greenfield for her 2006 photography book *Thin.* Is Brittany's desire for the diagnosis too grossly transparent for her to qualify as a real anorexic? But Brittany's in the *hospital,* and that has to mean something, right? There are standards, aren't there?

"I never had to go to the hospital or anything," my friend Kerry says over the telephone one evening. I've heard this rationalization from people many times before. I had asked Kerry about what I was like when I was sick, and then about her own disorder. Her response was a typically underplayed anorexic one.

"I was never really *sick* sick," she says. I stifle a laugh and roll my eyes, grateful that she can't see the look of utter dismissal on my face. I knew her when she wasn't well, and it was pretty apparent to anyone who had eyes that she was unhealthy.

"How could you have *not* considered yourself to have been, at least at one point, 'sick enough'?" I ask, incredulous.

"How could *you?*" is her understandable response to that.

When I was first found out, my therapist at the time told me I was a "mild case," but I was determined to show her—to show everyone—that I could be serious. To label an anorexic "not that bad" is to call him or her "normal," which is to say not sick at all, which is to say fat. And if getting to an arbitrary ideal weight or fainting or having a heart attack or being admitted to the hospital would make me feel like I was actually sick, then so be it. The hospital is what Kerry thought would have made her feel "*sick* sick." When that level of care is needed, it should be clear there's something wrong, no? For me, and for many, it wasn't enough. Upon each admission I was confronted with a bevy of girls thinner than I was, many looking to the person next to them, sizing her up.

"I don't deserve to be here," wail waifs in Craftmatic beds across the country. "*She's* so much worse than I am. So much thinner. I'm not that bad."

So maybe *that's* what makes a real anorexic: the refusal to believe in the actuality of one's illness. Consistently labeling one's self as exempt for one reason or another. Repeating ad nauseam, "I'm not that bad . . . I'm not sick enough." It's akin to the alcoholic credo that denial makes the diagnosis, though in this case, the word *diagnosis* implies more *accomplishment* than it does for an alcoholic, perhaps a little more codependency. Talk about a Chinese finger trap. The diseased person is in an abusive relationship with him- or herself, love and acceptance and sadism hopelessly entwined. The private language of the anorexic, though, absorbs both parts of the dialogue: the merciless, demeaning abuser and the dismissive, self-negating victim bent on securing the love and approval of the tormentor. A friend tells me she thinks she should get her uterus removed. It will help her maintain a lower weight, she says, and she doesn't think she'd be a good mother anyway. She doesn't want to subject a child to the kind of parent she's convinced she'd be: judgmental, rigid, obsessive. "But I was never really a serious anorexic," she follows in the same breath.

Or, as a nutritionist I once knew said, when comparing rationales, "When he hits me, he never leaves a mark."

So many people grasping for the title, refusing to believe they own it, writing exit clauses at the bottom of it, even stamping it on their foreheads without ever having come close to the heart of it. How many people *actually* have it? I mostly don't trust numbers, and the clinical definition has its holes, but I dutifully comb through the statistics in order to get a clearer idea of the prevalence of eating disorders in contemporary American culture. The only one I can find is offered by the Academy for Eating Disorders, and it is an appropriately vague and noncommittal statement.

"It is generally agreed that the incidence of eating disorders has increased over the last 30–40 years. Approximately 0.5 percent to 1.0 percent of late adolescent or adult women meet criteria for the diagnosis of anorexia nervosa."

One percent. So small. Such a coveted title. *I'll show them. I'll get there.*

• • •

WHAT WOULD ONE HAVE TO DO TO FEEL THOROUGHLY AND completely legitimized? The answer is: everything you believe the anorexia wants you to do, and if you're in an environment with lots of other anorexics, you need to do *better* than they do. This is one reason why it's nearly impossible to maintain a culture of recovery around anorexia.

"I didn't want to be the only one who had a good weekend," Ruby told me. She had recently been discharged into the day program, and we were standing by the nurse's station at Schneider Children's Hospital in January of 2003. She was smart and motivated and had decided to follow her meal plan, but at the last minute had fallen into the line of starving lemmings because she did not want to have to deal with the internal fallout that would ensue had she been able to check off the boxes next to breakfast, lunch, and dinner on her take-home menus. During breakfast at Schneider's, we patients were forced to state whether or not we had lost or gained weight. Often the careless supervisor would leave the notebook in which our weights were listed lying open on the table, and we would glance at one another frantically, hoping that someone would dive into a personal blitzkrieg and ask them to shut the book. Ruby was a victim of the insouciant atmosphere of this particular treatment program, the lightheartedness with which each person approached his or her after-hours weight-loss activities. The shrugs and smirks, the offhand "Oh, I *never* eat breakfast on the weekends." If Ruby didn't adopt a blasé, amused attitude toward her self-destruction, she wouldn't fit in, though the adolescent vernacular demeaned her pain. What would happen, really, was that there would be a barrage of criticism she would have to endure from the dictatorial board in her mind, a force that with each descent into the disease gains its own fortitude, knowledge, and identity. Ana or Ed are common pet names given to the disorder by teenage girls, and while I do not advocate bringing levity to the situation

by cooing at the anthropomorphized diagnosis, it is occasionally helpful to distinguish the disease from oneself, to
think of it as a foreign body, even if there is little scientific
evidence to support the claim. Anorexia, me. Disease, person. It is much more productive to abandon this practice of
crediting it with nuance and purpose and think of it simply
as a disease when it comes to recovering. A cancer, a virus à
la *Outbreak*. Evil. Something that must be stopped.

Ana screams at Ruby, "You already gained too much
weight in the hospital!" Ana minimizes the damage that can
be done over one weekend of dieting by saying, "It's not a
big deal. You can take it slowly in the real world. Work up
to healthy eating. Next weekend, you can do better." Ana
seduces her with a promise of *just one pound*. "Come on,"
she whispers, "just a little bit. It would be so easy." Ana waters
the seeds of paranoia in her head. "Don't listen to your
ex-roommate, Jane, when she offers support. She just wants
you to get fat. She wants to be the skinniest one here." Ana
warns her of the humiliation she is to face come Monday if
she has to record that her weight went "up," a cacophonous
note in a minor-key chorus of "downs."

Ana says a lot of things to those she visits. Ana knows
exactly what to say because she's inside one's cranium, privy
to all the necessary information. She knows how to get you
into that (twin-sized) bed and is aware when your priorities
and aesthetics change. One day the goal is to be "emaciated,"
the next to be "delicate." One day you are to starve yourself
to death, the next you are just losing a few pounds to look
good in a bikini. Anorexia is malleable, a folkloric shape-

shifter, constantly adapting, acquiring new vocabulary, new tricks, some of the most sophisticated of which come directly from therapeutic techniques or environments. When the anorectic is admitted to a hospital—a hierarchical world in which he or she can speak in the argot of calories and serving sizes and grams of fat, later the Quiet Room and CCs and NG tubes and metcarts—he or she is in some sense comfortable because this world is so neatly organized and predictable, and value is placed on all the things the anorexic places value on (namely, food, weight, and symptomology). For acute anorexics, everything becomes a means for measurement. The disease might as well parrot Twyla Tharp. In her book *The Creative Habit,* the famous choreographer writes: "Everything is raw material. Everything is relevant. Everything is usable." To us in the hospital, being ill was an art, and the unit a kind of dorm for Rhodes Scholars kids at Oxford University. Most everyone was worried that they would fall behind.

Anorexia is not only innately devious but also twice as easy to deny than other behavioral or addiction problems. Why? Anorexia is based upon *absence,* not substance. A nutritionist, a former bulimic, told me that she believed the treatment adage that bulimia was easier to overcome than anorexia. "At least I had physical proof of my illness, i.e., MY VOMIT," she wrote. Alcoholics and drug addicts live amid the paraphernalia of their dependence: empty bottles, syringes, pipes, charred tin foil. Anorexics have nothing but their changing silhouettes. They have blurry diagnostic lines and "issues with food," which are practically universal. How can one's identity be based on something so blissfully intent upon nothingness?

And just like most mentalities based on fear and blind devotion, anorexia is well suited to organization around the respect of a monster, and thus we have the pro-ana movement, a kind of nebulous death cult in which every member is his or her own personal and omnipresent demagogue.

Pro-ana accordions out to "pro-anorexia" and refers to a large swath of materials, mostly disseminated via the Internet, about anorexia, the acceptance of it (in relative terms) and disclaimers about such. These materials are often organized and condensed on personal websites, blogs, MySpace pages, or LiveJournals. (Facebook, once prime real estate for pro-anorexics, has declared that "such pages violate the site's terms of service agreement by promoting self-harm in others" and now works vigilantly to remove them. Tumblr and Pinterest have followed suit.) The sites fall somewhere on a general spectrum from the crude (maintained by the younger, less grammatically refined and less defensive about doling out the anorexic label) to the more sophisticated (maintained by those with more years of practiced illness, containing more emotionally melodramatic, quasi-poetic material, staunchly worded disclaimers, and a few verbal nods toward treatment and recovery).

According to a June 2010 study of pro-anorexia websites in the *American Journal of Public Health,* only 9 percent required a password or approved entry, and about half were "mostly graphic and written at a less than 8th-grade reading level." So while some webmistresses (a vast majority of the sites' owners are female) like to claim that they warn

viewers fairly, gaining entrance isn't exactly like breaking
into Fort Knox. In the introductory writings to the more refined sites, prologues on pages decorated with weeping angels or sad gothic androgynous creatures beneath blazing
banners that read WARNING—ENTER WITH CAUTION, many
authors state positions on eating disorders that are often pal-
pably ambivalent. They fiercely deny that one can develop
an eating disorder by viewing the material within, but they
don't give an alternative purpose to publishing it. One Internet scribe writes, "Anorexia is NOT a diet. Bulimia is
NOT a weight-loss plan. Eating disorders are serious and
dangerous and they are not something you can catch or
learn. This site does not, in any way, intend to encourage
any person to travel down the road of eating disorders."
Many of these writers purport to have full-blown anorexia
themselves—though a vast majority, according to pioneering
research by the University of Pennsylvania's Rebecka Peebles, are self-diagnosed. They believe themselves to be
"career" anorexics, way beyond the "recruitment" stage, to
borrow terms from Jacobs Brumberg's *Fasting Girls*. Most
of these site designers claim that they simply offer a place
where others can go to communicate openly and without
judgment about the disorder, something "pro-recovery"
sites do not allow, as they censor the language a writer uses.
(Stating your weight or the number of calories you eat in a
day, for example, is "not recovery talk" and grounds to be
banished from some e-communities.)

On the cruder sites, ones less likely to be guarded by
such intensely constructed (though ultimately pointless) ver-

bal moats, one can find a more direct declaration of a desire to become or remain anorexic, or a refusal to admit that there's anything wrong with wanting to starve yourself. There are often more visual aids here, pictures of the abdomens of models, their dresses hiked up beneath their flat chests, a seething caption beneath the image reading, "Your stomach isn't growling—it's *applauding*." These sites do not dissuade the viewer so much from perusing, but on neither end of the spectrum is there an explicit invitation to join the cabal. After all, if an aspiring (or actualized) anorexic invited others to follow suit, she would be inviting them to join the negative marathon, thus creating more competition for herself. *The thinner is the winner,* and the fewer people striving for thinness, the fewer opponents you have to worry about. Even girls who seek partners in starvation, a fairly common practice these days, do so I suspect mainly because competition is a motivating factor, not because they have any genuine "empathic" interest in the weight loss of their ana partner.

Most pro-ana websites include the following: dieting tips, suggested reading (for further dieting techniques), and thinspiration or "thinspo," which refers to pictures of very sick people or very slim Hollywood actresses (of course, Kate Moss and Nicole Richie are favorites) designed to motivate the viewer to lose weight. The noncelebrities whose pictures are posted on these sites are often superstar anorexics, women famous mainly, if not only, for their anorexia: the Kendall twins of Britain, for example, Karen Carpenter, Catherine Dunbar, or newer blogging sensations, twins

Maya and Eliza Koplowitz (anorexia loves an identical pair for the strict compare-contrast opportunity it provides). These tips are supplemented by a list of maxims known as the "Thin Commandments," which include mandates such as "Thou shalt not eat fattening food without punishing thyself afterward." This list was co-opted from the respected director of an eating disorders treatment clinic and former anorexic who wrote of her gratitude for her illness in the acknowledgments of *Your Dieting Daughter: Is She Dying for Attention?*: "And finally, last but not least, I am indebted to my own suffering, battle and victory over an old enemy *and* friend, anorexia nervosa, without whom I would not be the person I am today." Many sites have message boards where the like-minded can discuss issues related to starvation with one another. *How do I get rid of a hunger headache? What's the most effective brand of laxative? What's your favorite ana mantra?*

A telling study from the University of South Florida in 2007 found that "those who had a history of viewing pro-ana websites did not differ from those who viewed only pro-recovery anorexia websites on any of the study's measures, including body mass index, negative body image, appearance dissatisfaction, level of disturbance, and restriction."

Why would these viewers have similar reactions to these categorically different websites? Because when it comes down to it, "category" might be one of the few ways in which they are distinct from one another. Indeed, the 2010 study headed by Peebles found that most all the websites, despite their stated stance and intention, contained similar material. Webmasters and -mistresses are aware of this, it seems. They make sure to declare their sites as "pro-ana" or "pro-recovery" on the opening page because in many cases it won't be clear from the content. When I was a teenager, there was one well-designed eating disorders "support" site, decidedly and loudly pro-recovery, that became my portal into the world of anorexia on the Internet. It advised where to get help and had a simulacrum of a graveyard for those who had perished, but it also had a recommended reading list, chat rooms, and the occasional article, complete with statistics, on someone who was in the depths of the illness. The support forum was where I talked to other anorexics, commiserated about how much I hated my body, validated my sad-girl habits: *You do that, too!* The only thing missing, though I might have just neglected to notice that section, was the visual thinspiration. The restrictions about what could and could not be said were easy to get around: people would privately e-mail one another to get into the nitty-gritty. Someone would write introducing herself, beating around the bush before getting to it: "So, how many calories do *you* eat in a day? How do *you* get around weigh-ins?" The pro-ana movement wasn't "real" then; though some observers mark its beginning in the late 1990s, it didn't have a name or an overwhelmingly visible presence until the early aughts, nor did it declare itself with red bracelets or an argot of cartoonish pet names as it does now. Instead, it existed in this subtler and perhaps more insidious way.

"If you are looking to get anorexia or bulimia, please leave this website immediately," writes anorexic webmistress

FlawedButterfly. "You will not find this information within."

But you will find a list of low-calorie recipes, a height and weight chart, a link to an e–calorie counter, and a list of things to do to distract yourself when you're feeling hungry, which seem to me the exact tools one would need to cultivate bad habits. This site author has another website in which she emphatically denies that you can "catch" an eating disorder from the Internet. She is one of the more literate writers and ergo, one of the more hyper-defensive. She balks at the idea of people searching for an "ana diet" on the Internet, but has a whole section devoted to diets referred to as exactly this, including the onetime diet of the notorious Marya Hornbacher.

It seems, in theory, a pretty silly protest: why would a practicing anorexic need dieting tips, after all? Both pro-recovery and pro-ana advocates seem to ignore one key thing about anorexia, and that is this: the body reacts biochemically to starvation by releasing endorphins, which can make a person feel good and which can become pleasurable and emotionally addictive without discrimination, much like drugs or alcohol. (No one is totally certain as to how physically addictive starvation is.) There are factors that make some more prone to developing an eating disorder than others, and certainly not every wannarexic will develop anorexia, but it is not in the realm of the divine and unreachable gift that many would like to believe it is.

Take the oft-cited Minnesota Starvation Experiment spearheaded by scientist Ancel Keys in 1944. Keys took thirty-six men and put them on a semi-starvation diet for six months. Then he watched as the men's bodies and psyches deteriorated and they began to exhibit what is now considered classic anorexic behavior: developing food rituals, taking an agonizingly long time to eat, collecting recipes, feeding others, becoming irritable, losing ambition, and on and on. One of the participants, Daniel Peacock, described his attitude toward the experiment as one of fervency and deep spiritual commitment, in many ways how people describe their connections to faith and also to anorexia. "The experiment kind of became our religion in a way," he said in a June 2005 interview with the *Journal of Nutrition*. "And we were keeping the faith with that. And that was a pretty big job. So I think it would be fair to say that during that year that experiment was almost our religion. That's what we were dedicated to."

"I don't starve because I can," writes pro-anorexia webmistress TiNY TESSA. "I starve because I must. Anorexia is simply a necessity."

And even though those men at the University of Minnesota could have easily cheated on their diets, all but three of them were so dedicated to their cause that they didn't. Participant Harold Blickenstaff said of temptation in the *Journal of Nutrition* interview: "I had just decided that this was what I was going to do and so I was going to do it . . . Walking by a bakery was like walking by a bank. It might be nice to have what's in there, but it's out of the question." The retort to the argument that everyone could starve if properly motivated will obviously be that these men stopped depriving themselves immediately once the study had concluded, but many participants describe the structured rehabilitation period to have been the more difficult part of the study, and the expected full-recovery time was anywhere from two months to two years (this after a semi-starvation diet of about 1,800 calories, which is more than many anorexics would dream of consuming).

Nigerian playwright and poet Wole Soyinka wrote an essay while in prison in his native land, during which time he fasted to protest the civil strife there. His poignant and lyrical piece reads much like the statements of devotion on pro-ana sites, though his writing is decidedly more refined and beautiful. He describes becoming anxious to assert his power of will, and refusing to even drink water, instead cheating when they push the glass to his lips. (He means "cheat" in the anorexic way, i.e., pretend to drink but not actually imbibe.) Soyinka even experiences that joy that comes from noticing another's concern. He describes the masochistic pleasure derived from hunger pangs, and the sick glee he gets from watching the jailers eye him suspiciously. He closes with words that have found a faint echo in the Thin Commandments, a list of declarations often found on pro-ana sites: "I desire nothing."

"When young women get into the grips of this disease, their thoughts become very distorted, and part of it is they believe they're unique and special," said Ellen Davis, then clinical director of the Renfrew Center in Philadelphia in a 2002 *New York Times* article about the pro-ana movement entitled "The Way We Live Now: 9-8-02: Phenomenon; A Secret Society of the Starving." But they're not special, really; they're just physically reacting to starvation the way any *body* could.

It is, then, just as Naomi Wolf said, "It was dead easy to become anorexic."

Like many societies, loosely formed or otherwise, the pro-ana world has its own vernacular. The webmistress FlawedButterfly has a helpful list of translations for those of us less familiar: the standard pro-ana/recovery; thinspiration, or thinspo for short; Ana or Ed, etc. One she has left out, though, is *wannarexia,* a term I first encountered in a small story in one of the free morning New York City newspapers. The piece was about a high school counselor who had treated a young student with anorexia, but after he had her admitted to a treatment facility, he was faced with his next patient: a classmate of this anorexic who said she wanted to be sick just like the other girl.

Wannarexia is exactly what it sounds like: an amalgam of the words *want* and *anorexia.* Like pro-ana, wannarexia, is difficult to comprehensively define, but it is *not* a clinical diagnosis. It is a cultural phenomenon, one most prevalent among young women who see anorexia as a means to thinness and also popularity or acceptance among their peers. Some of these people (could) once have been medically diagnosed as ED-NOS, or Eating Disorder Not Otherwise Specified, which means the patient exhibits disordered eating habits and an obsession with his or her weight but doesn't fit the full criteria for bulimia or anorexia. (The committee in charge of composing the latest psychiatric diagnostic manual, the *DSM-V,* succeeded in removing ED-NOS as a diagnosis because it is so widely applicable.) When one trolls it becomes clear that wannarexics are a much-maligned population, and that many people, most notably diagnosed anorexics but others, too, characterize them as wholly superficial, flippant, vapid, and clearly more interested in having the *reputation* of being anorexic than in legitimately acquiring the disorder.

The Urban Dictionary, an online reference of newly coined terminology and slang, gives two examples of typical wannarexics and things they may say or do. They are:

> Wannarexic 1: "omigod i didnt eat today and now i way 72 pounds, WWMKD? stay strong, ana luv!"

For the uninitiated, WWMKD stands for "What Would Mary-Kate Do?" a spin on the popular Young Christians' movement phrase "What Would Jesus Do?" Both are mantras designed to point one in the direction of a higher power (in this case, Mary-Kate Olsen standing in as the symbol for anorexia) in the face of a moral crisis.

AND

> *Girl 1*: "This girl just told me she was anorexic and might be hospitalized. She doesn't look skinny at all though?"

> *Girl 2*: "That girl just has wannarexia. She wears a size 0 and pretends that it fits, but she can't do up the zipper."

The difference, according to these wannapsychologists,

is that a wannarexic is (a) more likely to brag about his or her illness, (b) more likely to consciously depreciate what he or she actually eats, and (c) less likely to be skinny. The way I see it, (b) is legitimate; once someone has crossed over that invisible (though oddly noticeable to outsiders) line from *trying* to starve to regularly starving (from wannarexia and/or ED-NOS to anorexia) he or she does tend to exaggerate or overestimate what he or she has eaten as opposed to downplaying it. As for (c): not looking "skinny at all" should rarely if ever be a determining factor as to the severity of one's eating disorder. With bulimia, of course, there is even less correlation between appearance and physical health.

Point (a) is the toughest. The stereotypical anorexic, yes, wears baggy clothing and attempts to hide her slight frame and peculiar habits, but not *all* anorexics do this. For some anorexics their size, their illness, is a badge they're happy to have earned and to have others gawk at. (This would also undercut the *DSM*'s assertion that anorexics have a disturbance in body image; anorexics who dress in skimpy clothing to show off must, logic says, have some idea that they are noticeably thin.) There was a woman I met in a hospital, Julia, a thirty-something from Florida with a noticeable face twitch and a habit of manic close-talking. She was very underweight but pranced around the unit in a child's short-sleeved Paul Frank T-shirt and capri jeans that often dipped below her waistline to reveal the tops of her ilium bones. She was eventually reprimanded for wearing revealing clothing and, later on, for trying to convince another patient to help her escape out the laundry chute.

So let's not be so quick to condemn the wannarexic. The exhibitionism inherent to wannarexia can be a clumsy cry for attention or help. It can also be the expression of a real anorexic in her honeymoon phase: over the moon about her new lover, spilling random intimate details of their co-existence despite the complete bafflement or disinterest of the audience. Many of the girls I met while institutionalized, mostly in their early teens, still had that self-aggrandizing-publicist streak to their anorexia. They were eager for others to see them as ill, not only because the label/diagnosis of anorexia was desirable (which makes them wannarexic), but also because if others perceived them that way, as "so sick," they felt like better/worse anorexics and thus worthy of the treatment they were receiving.

Such idiosyncratic advertisements of pride, whether expressed online or in real life, may be a hapless youngster's only knowledge of anorexia; having grown up always knowing of the disease's existence, he or she may have developed the disorder thinking that the digital communal aspect is actually an inherent part of, a *symptom* of, anorexia itself. This, as far as I can tell, is one of the only hard-and-fast ways to determine a "real" anorexic: if the disorder is developed with no prior knowledge of it whatsoever, the person is undoubtedly a "real" anorexic. But where could you find such a person in America nowadays? Or anywhere, for that matter?

Many of the articles about wannarexia that I have encountered were frantic to point out the terrible insult this condition is to those who are "actually" ill with anorexia. Talking to a reporter from the *Associated Press*, a young woman from the United Kingdom who runs a web forum for anorexics seethes, "Wannarexia is extremely offensive to those with anorexia and similar eating disorders. People who have eating disorders suffer." This statement deserves a closer look. For example, can someone "suffer" from wannarexia? I believe so. Unfulfilled desire can be immensely painful, object of desire notwithstanding. I imagine that the resentment felt by diagnosed anorexics toward wannarexics would be, if quantifiable, similar to the way someone with a disease such as breast cancer or lupus might feel toward someone who is anorexic or bulimic. A person with lupus, after all, has no control whatsoever over her disease, whereas an anorexic is ultimately the one in the driver's seat. Her illness, and her recovery, is, in the end, up to her.

The wannarexia phenomenon shouldn't shock us. Most anorexics can tell you stories of doctors or acquaintances or friends who only half-joke, voices tinged with envy, that they wish they had that problem. Some anorexics and bulimics, myself included, said these things before we got sick. Our society at large, if not only the microcosm of adolescent girls, a fierce and strange scorpion commune, values slenderness above all. It seems logical that one might desire a problem that seems, on the surface, only to make you really thin. As tributes to and cautionary tales of this disease become ever more accessible, youths are numbed to it and the most devastating of its effects, thereby allowing them to view potential repercussions (heart attack, osteoporosis, esophageal tears, and so on) as picayune parts of an admirable anorexic whole.

So what is the difference between wannarexia and anorexia? Is it wanting the disorder? The pride in the diagnosis? The secret desire to be hospitalized? No, as these things are abundantly present in acute cases of anorexia, too. Instead, imagine wannarexia as a gateway drug for teenagers, whose brains, numerous studies have concluded, are developmentally more inclined to make rash choices. For some, the first drink is just that; for others, it's the ticket to board the train to full-blown alcohol addiction. The same is true of anorexia: a young girl goes online, she reads a book in which dramatic things happen to the intelligent, wispy narrator, she tries out this aberrant behavior that she knows is *wrong,* that communicates how *little* she cares, she takes a few laxatives and skips a few meals, and *bam*—she ends up with her legs dangling off your hospital cot during winter vacation, crying as she's told that at this point, she's almost considered "chronic."

Only then might she pause and wonder: is that a label I ever wanted to wear?

At thirteen, I was a wannarexic. I admit to this with a good deal of shame. The term hadn't been coined yet, so I was only occasionally called out for "doing it for attention" or "being selfish," both of which were true. I scoured the Internet for diet tips and signed into recovery support forums using screen names like "losing myself fast" or "ChubbyGirl183." I whined about my weight gain (or lack of loss) and commiserated with my anonymous friends after eating a forbidden food or bingeing. I ate nothing around my friends but binged often, stealing French fries from my babysitting wards, choking down chalky cookies, my stomach grinding against the rim of my pants. I shoved objects—my finger, spoons, toothbrushes—down my throat repeatedly and was crestfallen to find that I had a supremely insensitive gag reflex. I told no one about these binges because I was deeply ashamed or because I wanted to be seen as solely anorexic. Or both. I wanted to look not just thin, not bikini-ready, but *sick,* visibly malnourished, as the idea was, to a degree consciously, to make my outsides match my insides: ugly, shriveled, and sad. I wanted to have a heart attack, be institutionalized, and become widely known for my intractable illness. The more I failed to achieve this, the more I chased the diagnosis, because it seemed that only that would absolve me of my sins, or put them into context retroactively. "She was acting all crazy, binge-eating, cutting, et cetera, and then she became *anorexic.*" It would all make sense then. Nice, neat little package.

But I got what I wanted and it *still* didn't make sense, and the further it went, the less sense it made. This, I believe, is the height of anorexia's fiendishness. Over the next ten years, my affection and desire for the disease steadily declined while my active dependence upon it grew. I went from desiring it at thirteen to fantasizing about a pill that would make my symptoms vanish at twenty-five. I didn't care about gaining weight. I didn't want people to think I looked "too thin." I just wanted to be *normal* and *healthy,* those things I once dreaded so much.

"I just can't do it by myself," I would weep meekly to my closest of confidantes. And it really *felt* like that, like there was something horrible inside me for which I was not entirely responsible but had nurtured over the years, something that by now had enough of its own momentum to roll over and crush my tired little body.

In high school I sat down at a lunch table with a plate defiantly devoid of anything nutritious and pushed slices of cucumbers around in big, slow circles; in college, I locked myself alone in my room with a bagel and tearfully begged myself to just. bite. down. At fifteen, I savored almost every comment about my emaciated appearance. Eight years later, I braced myself whenever I saw someone sizing me up.

"Starving-artist diet, huh?"

Shut up shut up shut up, I begged in my head.

At thirteen, I was a wannarexic. At twenty, the year of my last hospitalization, I was decidedly *not,* but the desire wasn't wholly eradicated. If you do something, doesn't that mean you want to, in at least some small way? In addition to the thousands of tiny, torturous rumination loops my malnourished brain got stuck doing, I was forced to contend with a larger, more philosophical question on which hung, I felt, my fate: did my wanting the disorder prior to its materialization constitute omniscience, or damnable premeditation?

CHAPTER 6

BLURRY LINES

PEOPLE WHO MAY ALSO HAVE BEEN CONSIDERED "WANNAREXIC" or "anorexic" or both:

1. ISABEL, MY MIDDLE SCHOOL FRIEND WHO SPENT MOST OF eighth grade pouting at her reflection in the bathroom mirror.

"If I had to describe myself using one adjective, it would be *sultry*," she cooed.

She asked me to buy her laxatives one day and the next chastised me for complaining when people made a "big deal" out of my eating habits. After my first hospitalization, she peppered me with questions. How much weight *had* I lost?

"You know what I thought of when I first heard you had gone there? I thought that maybe if I did that, people would stop expecting so much of me."

At the time I found this *horribly* offensive. How could she imply that I would have put myself and my family through so much just to coast for a while? But I also knew that there was some truth to it. I was sick partially because I wanted out of school and field hockey and other activities I didn't care much for, and terribly guilty for having that manipulative agenda. I wouldn't have been the first to use anorexia as a way to call in sick from life. Cherry Boone O'Neill, the daughter of folksinger Pat Boone, recalls in her memoir *Starving for Attention* that she began purging as a teenager to convince her parents she was actually sick so she could avoid attending high school. Malingering, essentially, led her to severe bulimia and anorexia.

When Isabel and I encountered each other years later, both sophomores at the same prestigious university, her clenched teeth and bag of powdery party favors mirrored that thing in me, a *desire for an out* that made my manifested anorexia not really any different from her wannarexia.

2. MOLLY FROM AN ARTICLE ABOUT ANOREXIA AND ISSUES OF control and blame in Britain's *The Independent* on April 1, 2007.

"Francesca and her daughter, Molly, understand better than most. Molly developed anorexia at the age of thirteen, almost deliberately, she says. 'I wanted to get out of this controlling relationship I had with my mother,' she says. 'I almost thought, "I know, I'll develop anorexia." Then it spiraled into a serious illness.'"

Operative word: *develop*.

3. JENNIFER. ONE DAY, A NEW GIRL APPEARED IN SILVER HILL'S living room.

"Who's that?"

"Jennifer," my friend Laura responded. "She's thirteen. She's here for cutting and depression, but they put her in this group because she wasn't eating or whatever."

Laura didn't seem convinced, and I said so.

"Yeah, I don't think she has an eating disorder."

Jennifer sat in a corner of the room, gnawing on her nails. Her eyes darted rapidly from girl to girl. Her skin and hair were the same sallow yellow, but nothing about her frame shouted poor nutrition. She wore her hair in a high ponytail, and the sleeves of her red sweatshirt were rolled up to her elbows, perhaps to display the large, raw scars that ran horizontally up and down both forearms.

When the therapist asked Jennifer why she was there (always the first question), she launched into a rapid, cloying monologue. "My dad is really worried about me because I never eat, and so are my friends because I always throw my lunch away at school and at home I feed it to my dog and all I eat are apples, and my therapist said I was really bad."

The following group was about "eating behaviors." The therapist handed us a worksheet. The first section was titled: "Eating Behaviors I Have." It listed a number of typical anorexic/bulimic behaviors done to prolong the process of eating, examples being: shaking your feet, cutting food into small pieces, counting to certain numbers before swallowing, and so on. The second section listed tactics to improve these behaviors. The therapists assumed that because it was all in front of us, we would give equal weight to the entire sheet. It took our undivided attention and faith for granted, which you should never do with (a) children or (b) people who are mentally ill.

When we were finished, we shared. Jennifer had checked every box in the first section. At dinner that night, she took her fork and knife, drew her elbows back quite far, and dramatically sliced at the spaghetti. She was told repeatedly to stop, but she only stared blankly at the supervisor. Instead of eating, she made a big show of pushing the clumps of cut-up spaghetti around her plate. It was her first and last day in the eating disorders program.

"We shouldn't have to see that," someone said. "Especially because it's so obvious that she's just doing it for attention."

I heard some time later that she tried to hang herself in her closet with her shoelaces, which didn't hold.

An early reader once asked me why I disapproved of Jennifer so much: "Her biggest crime, after all, is spaghetti." As I considered this, I realized that there wasn't much I could point to to distinguish Jennifer from the rest of us, the "real" ones, save a few extra pounds and a more apparent exhibitionism. I recall throwing nasty comments her way as she performed her noodle massacre, but it wasn't just me. The whole group had pounced on her and decried her actions, especially after she left. Recently, I e-mailed Laura to ask if she remembered Jennifer.

"Ah, yes," she wrote back, "I do remember Jennifer!

What a nut! I remember being so mad at her for just that, being a wannarexic. It was like, we are all here trying to get help and struggling through our meals, and you're going to come in . . . 'act out' and say you're one of us?"

Still, how does this make Jennifer any different? Was it the transparency of her desire? The clumsiness of it? The immediate and seemingly prideful openness? And are these things that she could have, with time and practice, learned to eradicate?

Definitely.

4. "I ALSO REMEMBER A GIRL NAMED ANNIE," LAURA CONTINUED. "She was nutso and what I would call a 'wannarexic.' I have a very foggy memory of her. She had been admitted for bulimia, but once there, she began acting like and saying she was anorexic. I remember us thinking she was full of shit. In groups she would wait for people to talk first and then just repeat what we all said in her own words as if they were her own experience."

I remember Annie, too. I was about to be discharged from the program when Annie came around. I was near my target weight and felt unhappy with my shape, but I didn't think I would ever have the willpower to lose the "extra" pounds again. I figured I would continue to gain forever, as if food had some sort of cumulative effect, although of course I knew otherwise. Because I felt it was time for me to leave the safe hospital bubble, I was doubly bitter toward those who were giddily wrapped up in their illness, as Annie was. Annie talked a big talk, and had claimed her doctor (outside the hospital) wanted to send her to a six-month residential program because all she ate were peaches. She would demonstrate how she and the other girls at her Catholic school liked to roll up their skirts while splaying her flabby legs in a decidedly unladylike fashion during groups. She laughed when the nurse told her to sit properly. Her laugh was too bawdy, her strawberry blond hair too thick, her arms too plump. Maybe this was it? This discrepancy between how you claim to feel (self-loathing, deathly insecure) and how you behave (confident, immodest)?

My whole life, I have been nearly pathologically photophobic, so I have very few pictures of myself past the age of twelve; because of this, I can't look to anything to prove or disprove my theories about the way I looked between thirteen and sixteen years old. Around the time Annie was there, though, we had a group at Silver Hill about photographs. The therapist offered to take a picture of any patient who wanted one, and then the patient could discuss with the group what she saw in the picture. Those who refused could talk about another time when they saw themselves in a photo and how it made them feel. When it was my turn, I told the group that I had recently come across a picture my mother had taken of my brothers and me when the four of us went on a trip to London. It was from two years earlier, when I was fourteen, before I had begun to seriously restrict, and so I was at a normal weight but carrying around with me always very intense body shame. That whole vacation, we had eaten in American chain restaurants like TGI Fridays or the Hard Rock Café because my brothers and I were picky eaters, and I was horrified that I had gone all the way to London to eat plates of French fries.

In the photo, I told the group, my brothers and I were standing in a very green park. The grass was so perfect it could have been a golf course. I was wearing my favorite black stretchy pants and a light coat, and was half-grinning at the camera. I had felt horrible, I told them, at the exact moment the camera snapped the picture, and yet when I looked back at it, I was amazed to see that I was thin! I was thin then! I related my epiphany with real joy and relief; many other therapeutic realizations I had delivered as if they were lines from a script, but this one felt true and good to say.

"So maybe," I ended, "if I was thin in the park in London when I was fourteen, maybe I'm not fat now even though I believe I am?"

I had been looking down during my speech, and when I raised my head, I looked directly across the room at Cindy, the one and only compulsive eater (nonpurging type) I had met in my six months at Silver Hill. Cindy was in her forties and obese, with short, grayish hair. A few errant whiskers poked out of her fleshy chin. She tried to be funny at the table as we ate, but we could tell she hated all of us. As I stared at her, tears streamed down her face, but when the therapist asked her why she was upset, she wouldn't answer. The next day, she asked to be transferred out of our group, and when we walked by her in the dining room, we would hear her telling her new friends the drug addicts the stories about all the "string beans."

Of course, we all believed she was just jealous.

5. Emma Simmonds, also at Silver Hill, tall and gawky with a deep voice and a short mane of brown hair. When she arrived, we started to tell her about Kristin's theatrics, and she immediately retorted with her own vita: she had been on life support, her doctor had come to visit because it was thought Emma would die, and on and on.

"Well, I was on a tube when I was twenty pounds less than her and I'm five-ten!" she gloated. Later, I mentioned her to my hospital therapist, who had also been assigned to Emma's case.

"She brags a lot," I said.

"Well, I think she's full of shit," the therapist responded.

6. Ramona, a friend of Lisa's, who was a roommate of mine at Silver Hill. Someone in the general adolescent psych day program said she knew Lisa and Ramona from school.

"I heard that Lisa chick is *weird*," she said, scrunching up her face. "She and her friend Ramona used to be, like, anorexic together."

When I asked Lisa, she told me that they had dieted together, encouraged each other.

"Ramona was really bad at one point. She went days [without eating] and passed out at track practice. But then she just stopped and . . ."

"You didn't?"

"I didn't."

Does this mean the label "wannarexic" could have applied to Lisa, ghost-pale, textbook-malnourished Lisa, at some point or another? And when did Lisa cross over from wannarexic to anorexic? Between hospitalizations two and three? If you never claim to "want anorexia" but decide to embark on a ninety-calorie-a-day diet lifted from the pages of an anorexic's memoir, are you wannarexic? If you become ill subsequently and are hospitalized numerous times, does the sin of wanting it become thus absolved?

7. A FEW DAYS INTO MY SECOND STAY AT CORNELL IN 2004, a new girl arrived. The long-faced doctor stood next to her at the threshold of the dining room, where we sat drinking our liquid supplements.

"This is Ashley," he said.

She was wearing flannel pajama pants, sneakers, and a fleece pullover, and had obviously been crying a good deal: her eyes were red and puffy, and snot wetted the bottom of her nose like dew. Her hair was ruler straight and piss blond, and the rest of us did the requisite up-and-down and breathed a sigh of relief. Solid limbs, small paunch. Nothing by which to be intimidated.

The first night Ashley was there, I heard her ask another patient if she thought the staff would let her bring in her thinspiration journals.

"Your *what?*" the patient asked, clearly unaware of what thinspiration was.

"My thinspiration journals. My notebooks where I paste pictures of models and skinny people so I can be motivated to lose weight."

The other patient just stared back silently for a minute.

"You're in a hospital. So no. I don't think they will," she said, deadpan.

Ashley offered an excuse for her robust form, a slight variation from those I had heard from myriad other normal-weight hospital patients, anxious about being the healthy-looking fish in a sea of scrawny minnows. "Two weeks ago, I was a size double zero," she told anyone who would listen. "Everyone was always threatening to fatten me up, so I just did it myself." We rolled our eyes and among ourselves we doubted that she had ever been a regular zero, let alone a *double* one.

Ashley embraced her superficial-teenager persona with gusto.

"I like things because they're popular!" she announced sincerely during a group. "I like guys who are buff!"

When her favorite pop song came on the radio ("1985" by Bowling for Soup), she would blare the volume and dance maniacally around the living room until the nurses told her to turn it down and sit.

"But it's my *soooooong*," she whined.

During visiting hours one day, a friend of mine overheard a conversation between Ashley and her mother. Ashley's younger sister was also present.

"Maybe I should take away your stickers before you come home," Ashley's mother said meekly.

Ashley stood up, stomped her foot, and began to yell. "That is not fair! Don't you take away my Barbie stickers! *I am Barbie!*"

Ashley clearly equated anorexia with things like conformity and popularity. She wanted to be anorexic because being anorexic meant being thin and a cheerleader and a part of her high school's upper echelon. When she was admitted, she wasn't anorexic—or maybe wasn't anymore—but rather yearning to be. What effect does hospitalization have on someone like this? On a wannarexic?

8. JODI, A CHARACTER FROM AN ACQUAINTANCE'S MANUSCRIPT entitled *Pretty Little Actress,* which tells the story of the author's struggle with anorexia and inpatient hospitalization. The following describes Jodi, who was a patient at the same facility.

> Jodi was . . . special. She was desperately attention seeking, and none of us truly believed she had an eating disorder. Everything she said or did was an exaggerated mimic of something that one of us did. If someone didn't finish her meal, Jodi would refuse to touch a bite of her next one. If someone was caught exercising, Jodi would undoubtedly be jogging in circles around her room. It got to the point where she had to have one-to-one supervision—meaning that a staff member had to be within arm's reach of her at all times. She had to sleep on the sofa in the living room so she could be watched. She loved it. She relished telling everyone who visited that she was *so* sick she wasn't able to be trusted. She eventually stopped eating enough that the staff gave her a feeding tube, although I honestly think they did it to teach her a lesson.
>
> We couldn't stand her.

Not only was she making a compete mockery of a very real illness, but she was extremely needy and clingy. She was constantly getting chastised by the staff, repeatedly yelled at by one of the girls—but all this was attention, so she continued to do it. I personally tried to ignore her. I was of the opinion that she had not fully mentally developed, and while I felt bad for her, she drove me nuts. So when she volunteered to be the subject of a psychodrama [therapy group], no one was thrilled with the idea of participating.

[The therapist] was clever, though. She allowed Jodi to cast her psychodrama and tell her sob story (which changed every time she told it), but then she began calling her out on some of her behaviors.

"Why do you think you spend so much time breaking the rules?"

Jodi put on a pout. "I don't mean to . . . I just have such a hard time with the meals. I know I need to eat and get better, but it's just so hard." She was repeating something another patient had said earlier that morning.

I've seen this before, too, the verbal plagiarism of a fellow patient. I remember Kristin talking about a botched meal one evening during group and using verbatim a line Liz had weeks earlier, her cadence and rhythm exactly the same. "But . . . it . . . didn't . . . stay . . . down," Kristin said, parroting Liz exactly. I didn't say anything then because I thought it was sort of weird that I remembered that in the first place.

The author of this as-yet-unpublished memoir, who attended the same writing program as I did, was to me *without a doubt* a real anorexic. In her manuscript, she describes the beginning of her anorexia as a slow, almost imperceptible shift. She started going to the gym more and more often, and started eating less, and then less, and then next to nothing. She didn't stalk anorexia—the diagnosis, the symptoms, the tearful interventions—the way I had. She didn't want it; rather, it just *happened*. When I heard that she was also writing about anorexia, I immediately panicked. Not only was I sure that she was a "better" anorexic than I had ever been, but likely her writing was more cohesive, her thought process more elegant and sophisticated. I began to backpedal rapidly, thinking that perhaps the reason I took such a hard-nosed view on matters concerning writing and anorexia was because I knew that my statistics, if laid out plainly, would not be so impressive. *Give up,* said the little voice. *Give up now.*

After we had completed the writing program, the author contacted me and asked me if I wanted to swap manuscripts. I obliged, and when I came to the portion about Jodi, I expressed concern that I was just like that loathed patient: attention seeking, clingy, juvenile. The author responded quickly, "You are nothing like Jodi. At *all*."

But how does she know what lurks in my heart?

9. BEAUTYINTHEBONES, A WEBMISTRESS WHOSE WEB PAGE IS titled "I want to be the smallest I can be. When I see bones, that is the day I will feel free." Her site is chock-full of the

usual pro-ana information and tips, and also includes a personal diary section.

> Big News! I got tickets to *The Nutcracker* performed by the Moscow Ballet!!!!! I am SSOOO excited. I have to lose weight! I will feel so fat around all those skinny ballerinas but I have about 6 weeks to get ready. If I can't do it by then, then I just suck and don't deserve to be called anorexic and I'll have to delete this site. Which would be a horrific chain of events that I won't let happen lol :)

"Stay strong!" her readers encourage her.

"Stay strong!" we would tell one another, nervously hugging before going home from program for the weekend. Ostensibly we meant, "Follow your meal plan!" But what was "strong" to us? Not "recovery behavior," surely. Strength was equivalent to willpower, and "willpower," with regard to food, means abstinence, no matter what.

10. A READER WHO RESPONDS TO A *NEW YORK TIMES* WellBlog post entitled "The Troubling Allure of Eating-Disorder Books." OW writes:

> I was a teenager and college student in the 1990s, so I was exposed to a lot of educational and cautionary material on eating disorders. Honestly, the "education" did glamorize it for me, to the point that I tried to become anorexic (I never succeeded, as I apparently lacked the underlying pathology). It just seemed like a good and socially acceptable way to get

attention from adults and peers. (Starving yourself tends to earn sympathy, but eating too much and gaining weight just earns derision.) I resented the attention actual anorexics and bulimics received, and wanted to develop some kind of outward manifestation of my own stress, so people wouldn't just look at me and see a healthy, normal girl, but a girl in emotional need. Even if it doesn't lead to actual self-starvation, I think overexposing young women to information about eating disorders can lead to destructive behaviors and negative emotions.

May I add that drug and alcohol abuse, promiscuity, self-mutilation, and most other forms of teenage rebellion usually incite disapproval and scorn as well, or at least a wary eye toward the person's character, while anorexia tends to evoke sympathy. "Poor little perfectionist . . . so hard on herself."

11. AND ANOTHER RESPONSE TO THE SAME POST, BY RM

When I was about 11 years old, I was exposed to information regarding eating disorders in middle school health class and was totally intrigued with the topic. By the time I was 12, I was submerging myself in research—writing reports, watching movies, reading anything I could get my hands on that had to do with anorexia or bulimia. I wanted to be those girls. By 13, I had full-blown anorexia and was admitted into the hospital, just in time for Thanksgiving and the winter holidays. I was in 9th grade.

I'm 26 now and just got out of a residential program
following a terrible relapse. During this relapse, at my worst
point, I spent hours . . .full days and nights even . . . watching things online (movies, tv specials, video blogs, thinspiration), searching for tips, listening to Superchick's lyrics
and reading books like *Wasted*. I attribute the severity of
this relapse to the amount of information that is available
from the media, and I'm a grown woman.

There seem to be two types of wannarexics: those
who follow the "instructions" because they think they are
a means to a losing-weight end, and those who do it as a
means to a *diagnostic* end. RM's "I wanted to be those
girls" implies a desire to be underweight, but also for the
label itself and the spectrum of possible consequences, including but not limited to: diagnosis, stamped and approved; bone deterioration; heart problems, including
cardiac arrest; and hospitalization. It is a desire to be told
you are a person with a mental illness, something that, at
one point in time, would have offered little benefit except
a lifetime pass to a state hospital and a stigma within society. This strain of wannarexic thinking is similar to
Munchausen syndrome, which is a mental disorder that
causes sufferers to either feign illness or actually make
themselves sick in order to get attention. How conscious
of their goals they are is up for debate. (Munchausen is
sometimes colloquially referred to as "hospital addiction
syndrome.")

But how to satisfy the desire to be noticed and then

compartmentalized in such a way without causing irreparable damage to one's body and mind in the process?

12. WHEN I WAS TWELVE, I WAS IN THE CAR WITH TWO FRIENDS named Meredith and Kelly. Meredith said, "Kelly and I tried to be anorexic for a few days at camp, but it didn't work."

Still a lover of French fries and a hater of all typical teenage girl activities (makeup, bra shopping, boy chatter, dieting), I was appalled. "Why? Why would you do that?"

A year later, I was praying for some sort of Divine Liposuction.

Two years after that, I was in the local psych ward.

Two years after *that*, I ran into Kelly at a party and noticed her frame: a little *wrong*, a little *too thin*. My curiosity was piqued, but I didn't even need to bait her. She told me with little to no prompting that her parents had made her go to Overeaters Anonymous, which is a twelve-step group that, despite its name, serves people with all eating disorders. She didn't want to risk me thinking that she was there for something else, so she clarified, "It's otherwise known as *undereaters* anonymous."

13. JENNIFER EGAN, NOVELIST AND CONTRIBUTOR TO *GOING Hungry,* writes: "I first encountered the term at age thirteen, in 1976, in a magazine article about a girl who had starved herself for reasons no one understood. I remember her picture . . . I looked at her and felt my whole being contract into a single strand of longing. I wanted that: *anorexia.*"

14. RENEE CLOE, INTERVIEWED FOR AN ASSOCIATED PRESS article, "'Wannarexic' Girls Yearn for Eating Disorders" by Valerie Bauman.

> Renee Cloe, 40, remembers wishing she could be anorexic after watching a made-for-TV special on the subject.
>
> "I was a teenager and wanting to be thin, wanting to fit in," Cloe said. "And the thought was, if I could just get anorexia it would be easy, and that's a very wrong thought."
>
> For Cloe, that aspiration led to years of starvation dieting. She lost a lot of weight—her body-mass index fell below healthy levels—but was not treated for an eating disorder.
>
> "It's hard for me to say one way or another whether I was anorexic," Cloe said. "I was thin and miserable, but I was never diagnosed or put in the hospital. But, definitely, that early flirtation with it led to years of being messed up."
>
> Later on, she became overweight as she veered between binge eating and crash diets, eventually finding her way to a fit and healthy lifestyle as a martial arts enthusiast and personal trainer.

15. MICHAEL KRASNOW, ONE OF THE MOST FAMOUS MALE anorexics in the world. In his memoir, *My Life as a Male Anorexic,* which is terrifyingly spare and blunt, he describes how his anorexia developed from a suggestion. Krasnow, who was engaging in seriously obsessive behaviors such as relentless studying, was taken out of school by his psychiatrist. During a session one day, his doctor voiced concern

that Krasnow might replace his obsession with studying with a new fixation.

"This possibility had never occurred to me until he mentioned it. Dr. C put the idea of a new obsession into my mind. As a result, when I left school, I found myself thinking, 'Okay, Dr. C said I might end up with a new obsession; now, what can I do to replace the studying?' In other words, I made a conscious effort to find a new obsession."

He began to brush his teeth constantly until he made "the decision that would lead to anorexia," namely, that he wouldn't eat so that he wouldn't feel the need to clean his teeth so often. His starvation led him to be hospitalized and then diagnosed with anorexia. When told of his diagnosis, his reaction was one of pride.

> When I [told my doctor about feeling fat], he told me it was a characteristic of anorexia nervosa. "What's that?" I asked. When he explained the condition, I automatically labeled myself an anorexic. It's hard to explain, but it almost seemed "glamorous" to me (I don't know if that's the right word), something I wanted. I had an illness; I had something few others had; I was special. The anorexia gave me an identity and made me an individual.

Krasnow touches on an interesting point. Anorexia as a label has a strange allure that we don't associate with many other mental illnesses. Though not unheard of it, it would be decidedly more peculiar to hear a similar narrative for someone diagnosed with obsessive-compulsive disorder, for example, or depression. It was the prospect of a unique and specific identity—one that was focused on the pursuit of a goal—that spoke to him, and so he reached out and embraced it. His food behavior preceded his understanding of and *desire* for the illness, which would classify him as a real anorexic, but his admitted perception of the illness as "glamorous" and his eagerness to be diagnosed speak to the wannarexic in the most undeniably serious of cases. Because Krasnow died of starvation in 1997, we will never know why he felt that anorexia was "glamorous" or that it made him special.

16. DAPHNE MERKIN, CONTRIBUTING WRITER FOR *THE NEW York Times Magazine*. In her 2009 piece "A Long Journey in the Dark: My Life with Chronic Depression," she writes of her time in a psychiatric hospital:

> It wasn't only the anorexics' Ensure that I coveted. From the very first night, when sounds of conversation and laughter floated over from their group to the gloomy, near-silent table of depressives I had joined, I yearned to be one of them. Unlike our group, they were required to remain at lunch and dinner for a full half-hour, which of necessity created a more congenial atmosphere. No matter that one or two had been brought onto the floor on stretchers, as I was later informed, or that they were victims of a cruel, hard-to-treat disease with sometimes fatal implications; they still struck me as enviable. However heartbreakingly scrawny, they were all young (in their mid-twenties or thirties) and expectant; they talked about boyfriends and concerned parents, worked tire-

lessly on their "journaling" or on art projects when they weren't participating in activities designed exclusively for them, including "self-esteem" and "body image." They were clearly and poignantly victims of a culture that said you were too fat if you weren't too thin and had taken this message to heart. No one could blame them for their condition or view it as a moral failure, which was what I suspected even the nurses of doing about us depressed patients. In the eyes of the world, they were suffering from a disease and we were suffering from being intractably and disconsolately—and some might say self-indulgently—ourselves.

In the world of the general psych ward, the anorexics are the Gifted Program, or the Special Ed—never mind which, both get special treatment, their own classroom, and lots more care and attention than your average Depressive Daphne. The "enviable" visibility of their illness makes sense, the way it is considered real because we can *see* it. I continue to struggle with the belief that melancholia is meaningless unless you manifest it somehow; being visibly malnourished always seemed more effective and noteworthy than simply being depressed. What Merkin doesn't mention is that maybe some of these girls had developed anorexia as a way to assuage and manifest their own depression. She also doesn't note here the most terrifying thing about anorexia: if you aren't depressed before you get sick, there's a very good chance you will be once you're in it, and often the malaise sticks around even after you physically recover. A permanent chill from getting too close to death, from inviting it in, it "hovers behind the scenes . . . sits in the space behind your eyes, making its presence felt even in those moments when other, lighter matters are at the forefront of your mind," as Merkin writes. I often think of the explanation of suicidal thoughts offered by Susanna Kaysen in *Girl, Interrupted*. Kaysen writes that the real persistence of suicidal ideation is that suicide, once you have opened your mind to the possibility, becomes a potential solution to any and all problems. After you've considered it, you can never *stop* considering it.

Many people who find themselves at the better—physically healthier—end of anorexia wonder where their unfathomable melancholy came from. It becomes a chicken-and-egg question. Hornbacher theorizes that it's probably a little of both natural predisposition to depression and the long emotional hangover from anorexia, just as the psychiatrists and clinicians and research doctors usually say that the road to anorexia is paved both by your environment and your genetic makeup. It's an unsatisfying answer, but it's the best one we have, and after all, once you're stuck with the pains of Icarus, why bother dwelling on how you got them?

Like Merkin and Hornbacher, I exhibited spots of depressive behavior as a child, but would I be nearly as fixated on death now had I never coveted it? I doubt it. There is no way of determining this, though, as a doctor would need to evaluate my psyche prior to my illness, and if someone could have prophesied it, we'd presumably be able to avoid it.

17. CAROLINE KNAPP, WHO WROTE THE FOLLOWING IN HER book *Appetites,* which *Salon* called "the smartest anorexia memoir ever written."

> One morning, about eight months into my year of weight gain and weight loss, I sat at my desk reading a profile of an anorexic girl in the *New York Times Sunday Magazine.* I'd never heard the term "anorexia" before or the phrase "eating disorder," and I pored over the piece, read it straight through to the end then read it again. The woman in the profile was young, in her teens. Her weight had dropped to below eighty. She did thousands of sit-ups, late into the night, and she'd become so skeletal that her arms and belly had grown a soft dark downy fur called lunago [*sic*], a sign of the body's attempt to compensate for the lack of insulating body fat. I don't remember any other details, but I do remember my response, which was so peculiar I wouldn't quite identify it for many years: I envied her. I envied her drive and her focus and the power of her will, and I suspect I saw in this poor girl's sheer determination the outlines of a strategy: one anxiety (weight) as the repository for many anxieties (men, family, work, hunger itself); emaciated thinness as a shortcut of sorts, a detour around painful and confusing feelings, a way to take all hungers—so varied and vast—and boil them down to their essence, one appetite to manage, just one.

18. THREE SEVENTH-GRADE GIRLS WHO CAME INTO THE school nurse's office to visit a friend with a bellyache. I was

fifteen, just a month or so away from my first hospitalization, and I was spending my lunch period on the plastic cot nursing a can of Ensure. It was a particularly bad day. I felt chillier and more despondent than usual. I stared in the mirror at the bluish bags beneath my eyes and thought, *I look awful.* As I sighed and sipped, the seventh-grade girls piled on top of one another on the other cot, nudging at their nauseated friend. Their eyes drifted to the posters on the wall that students had made for Eating Disorder Awareness Month, which they were learning about in health class. The big white paper was decorated with pictures of skinny models cut out from *Vogue* and *Self.* Across the top was written in magazine letters, ransom note–style, "How Thin Is Too Thin?"

"I don't think it would be so bad to be anorexic," one of the girls announced. "I mean, as long as you weren't so bad you were going to die or something."

"You shouldn't talk about things you don't know," I reprimanded absentmindedly. A blond member of the group turned toward me. Her eyes drifted down toward my wrists.

"Is that a *special* drink?" she asked.

Did you just say that out loud? What an attention whore.

19. The aforementioned Brittany, an enthusiastic recruit, aged fifteen, profiled in the book *Thin.* Brittany writes:

> Then I went on the Internet for a checklist of what symptoms occur when you're anorexic or bulimic, and I went through them to make sure I had every single one so I could

be the perfect anorexic. I cut out the fat in my diet to miss my period. I tried to force myself to not sleep so that I could actually have sleep disturbance. I said I had constipation so I could get laxatives, which I kind of fell in love with. I looked at my checklist every day.

Brittany's path toward anorexia is emblematic of a re-markable shift in the way a disease develops. It's almost as if she's going *backward,* the actual diagnosis seemingly being the primary goal, and the secondary that of being thin, which is more traditionally seen as the bait that tempts the fish. In order to get what she wants, she must immediately and wholly embrace the disorder, its name, its ramifications. Oh, and have access to a checklist of symptoms, the deter-mination to develop behaviors that will make her exhibit them, and reason to think that they mean something, like "perfect" or "empty" or "wasted." *The Best Little Girl in the World.* And Brittany ends up in treatment, numerous times. So when is she actually anorexic? When she steps onto the grounds of the Renfrew Center? How many things on the list need to be checked off? When is there really a problem— when she decides that she wants to be anorexic or when she is formally diagnosed?

CHAPTER 7

TITILLATION

BRITTANY WAS ONE OF FOUR RENFREW CENTER PATIENTS profiled in depth in the book *Thin* by Lauren Greenfield, or, as I like to call it, "eating disorders porn."

"I've never seen a book with so many pictures!" online reviewers exclaim.

Greenfield is a California-based photographer whose breakthrough work was *Girl Culture,* an illustrated coffee table book of photographs of women and girls in various settings indigenous to them, such as cheerleading practice, a tanning bed, spring break, a high-end New York City clothing store. There aren't any of women in libraries, on college campuses, performing spinal operations, or presiding over board meetings, but I suppose that wouldn't be indicative of the female subculture that Greenfield would like us to believe is the most important. The pictures in the book are accompanied by written testimony by a twenty-year-old lingerie model, a number of Vegas showgirls, and summer residents of a weight-loss camp in upstate New York. One gets the impression that Greenfield fancies herself the Margaret Mead of contemporary American female culture, but this would be a stretch. After all, is it really "a powerful indictment of our cultural obsession with physical beauty" if it's just a simple exhibition of it? Where's the analysis or the potential angles from which to combat the aforementioned obsession? If Greenfield is interested in calling our attention to our "cultural obsession with physical beauty," then perhaps she shouldn't deal in exactly the currency—i.e., support the two-dimensional—that she presumably condemns.

In *Thin,* her follow-up to *Girl Culture,* Greenfield focused on the world of the Renfrew Center for Eating Disorders at its Coconut Creek, Florida, location and made a book and documentary film about what she observed. Greenfield profiled four girls, including Brittany and twenty-five-year-old Shelly, a psychiatric nurse from Utah who enjoys her job because she feels like she "really fit[s] in with the patients." At the beginning of the book, Shelly has a feeding tube in her stomach, which doesn't bother her so much because "getting a tube is a status symbol that you are really anorexic." That is actually a quote from another Renfrew patient, but Shelly agrees.

Shelly is visibly malnourished—she is *without a doubt.* She gives lip service to her bad body image, and yet she is a willing subject in Greenfield's project. In one photo, she lifts up her shirt to show the feeding tube inserted into her stomach just above her decorative belly button ring. I was surprised at the various states of undress the subjects are shown in throughout the book—I wouldn't have been photographed even with a bag over my head while I was sick, let alone half naked—before I remembered the exhibitionistic element present in many cases of anorexia, the bastard child of vanity and self-loathing. (See also: the episode of *Intervention* in which a severe anorexic stands in front of a mirror berating herself for being obese, yet proceeds to spend a majority of her time on camera in her underwear.) This is a facet of the disease that is often ignored or mistaken for progress or "sharing" the "deep secrets" and "shame" attached to the suffering. After all, isn't sharing *good?* Isn't that how one gets *better?*

But in reality, indulging the exhibitionist streak of anorexia does everyone a great disservice. To pay such attention to the body of an eating-disordered person (the number on a scale, her self-inflicted wounds, the pieces of paper on which she tallies her calories for the day are all things Greenfield liberally photographs) is to actually *reinforce* the belief that got her into that position in the first place. *It is my body that will do the talking. It is the language of my eating disorder that will speak the loudest.*

The term *porn* is, of course, short for *pornography,* which is defined as lurid, sensational material usually (but not always) of a sexually explicit nature. Another word to consider in the context of *Thin* is *provocation.* The bodies on display are meant to provoke a reaction from the viewer.

So what reaction is Greenfield looking to provoke by publishing *Thin*? Her introduction provides no real answer. Her language is pretty but vague, and reveals the project's lack of ambition: "The pathology of eating disorders is compelling, symbolic, and important to understand. It is extreme and atypical, but unlike other mental illness, it has a visible relationship to the values of mainstream culture." Translation: anorexics are the extreme example of our "society's unhealthy emphasis on our physiques." *For the Love of Nancy*, she's *thin!* Greenfield has here brought to light something we were all aware of and says virtually nothing new about it.

Two main groups would be interested in a project like *Thin,* and each is likely to have a specific, distinct reaction. The first set of individuals are those who are not eating disordered but have a vested interest in people who are: parents, loved ones of those afflicted, health care workers (though they are likely to learn little if *anything* from a text as facile as *Thin,* composed almost entirely of spectacular imagery to which they most likely have been exposed to the point of desensitization). The second group is those involved in or typically interested in eating disorders, namely eating-disordered people, wannarexics, and your garden-variety adolescent girls, many of whom are blindly weight obsessed and will mine any source related to the topic. Their reaction to this thinspiration is likely to be increased motivation. Greenfield's book and documentary, not surprisingly, are cited on a number of pro-ana websites. "Polly *died,*" one Internet scribe writes about another of Greenfield's subjects with barely concealed awe. "I've seen that documentary, like, 300 times."

The second demographic is easier to evaluate. Throughout the written testimony, anorexic and bulimic patients at the Renfrew Center unintentionally point out the obvious problems with the reductive project in which they are participating. "I used to love the books where I would read an anorexic story. I loved seeing the skinny women on TV and comparing their bodies to my body," Cheryl, thirty-five, from Missouri, writes. "I loved Karen Carpenter. I would get on the computer and stay all night and see how small she had gotten. She was my superstar."

Clearly those with anorexia (nascent, manifested, acute, wanna) will not be dissuaded by a coffee table book filled with large, pretty pictures of terribly thin bodies, some more repulsive than pictures of Karen Carpenter at her worst. The fact that Greenfield ignores this indicates that she knows that the more provocative the portraits, the more the book will sell. Not even the knowledge that Carpenter died is enough to dethrone her as an anorexic icon, nor is it enough to make young Polly Williams less a subject of fascination among consumers of *Thin*. In her death, too, Williams became the most "successful" anorexic of all those featured in *Thin*. Recall the treatment center maxim, invoked at least twice by girls interviewed: "The best anorexic is one who's six feet under." Death is the biggest and most final accomplishment. Everyone loves a juicy tragedy, and the fact that Greenfield banks on this is inexcusably selfish.

Joan Jacobs Brumberg, aforementioned professor of history and women's studies at Cornell University and author of *Fasting Girls,* provides the foreword for *Thin* and in it, acknowledges what she calls the "social contagion" factor of eating disorders. Brumberg expresses a hint of concern for both new superstar Cheryl and her audience:

> Perhaps, the patients were also disarmed and/or seduced by the potential to tell their individual stories to the world. Participation in a documentary project could give meaning to their prolonged suffering, either as a warning to others or as a way to legitimate their illness. All of these motivations are possible in a culture like ours where there is no longer any stigma attached to public narratives of deep despair and recovery.

And now Cheryl herself gets to be someone's Karen Carpenter, immortalized at an apex of her disease. For all those out there on the eating-disordered spectrum perusing the book, she becomes another paradigm of illness. She represents a level they ought to reach in order to feel "sick enough" or "good enough." So what Greenfield is doing, ultimately, is giving these very sick women a chance to be role models to young girls. What effect is this characterization *likely* to have on Cheryl? It could solidify the idea that anorexia is a part of her "identity," something over which anorexics express an extreme amount of anxiety. She could use the project in the future either to her advantage or her disadvantage. It could serve as a "look how far I've come," but maybe only if she tucks it away until her anorexia ceases to have a significant hold on her, which could take a long time, if it ever happens at all.

Let's compare Cheryl to Lori Gottlieb who published

a journal of her struggle with anorexia titled *Stick Figure*. Back in the summer of 1978, Lori was hospitalized in Los Angeles for malnutrition. She was eleven years old. At that time, anorexia wasn't a very common diagnosis, and Lori wasn't really aware of what it meant until her therapist instructed her parents to buy Hilde Bruch's *The Golden Cage,* generally considered to be the first serious book about anorexia by a clinician. Lori, who was precocious, read the book and decided it was "incredibly stupid," except for the part "when Hilde told stories about teenagers named Kate, Hazel and Karla who felt as lonely as [Lori] did." Lori saw in these other anorexic girls true comrades: girls who are smart and artistic and interested in things, as opposed to her classmates, who are cliquey and boring.

"Plus [Hazel and Karla] did smart things like wear weights under their sweatpants for their weight checks . . . Believe me, I never would have thought of that."

After she was admitted to Cedars-Sinai Medical Center, her physician, Dr. Gold, told her that he would like to use her as a case study, which would mean filming her and showing the tape to residents. He wanted to show her the finished product in the hopes that she would see how unhealthy she looked.

Then he said that I'm an "excellent case," which is why they picked me in the first place. I guess that means I'm an excellent dieter. I was thinking about how it means I'm the best dieter at my school, and I'm probably the best dieter in the country, maybe even the world! I mean, I must be, because they want to make a *movie* of me. I was pretty excited about it, but then I thought that maybe the doctors watching my film would have seen thinner anorexics than me . . . so I decided not to eat anything until after the filming tomorrow. Not one bite.

Lori, not surprisingly, oscillated between ecstasy at being deemed an "excellent case" and fear that she was "a pretty bad example." She refused to eat because she wanted to make sure that she lived up to her role. In the end, her doctor decided not to go through with the project. His reasoning? "He felt I got too excited about it, and it would just make me feel good about being emaciated.

"'But I'm an excellent case!' I said, then Dr. Gold said this was exactly why he wouldn't film me after all."

New Age lovers of expression and denouncers of shame might call me severe, but I believe that Dr. Gold made the right choice. He recognized that transforming Lori into a paradigm had an immediately negative effect on her psyche and, subsequently, her behavior.

Where is the Renfrew Center's Dr. Gold? Why didn't anyone there consider this possibility? Or at least recognize the fact that such a public announcement of illness is bound to produce ambivalence on the part of the anorexic, whose usual reaction to ambivalence is to force him- or herself to feel only one way, to grasp control—aka engage in eating-disordered behaviors?

When I was a freshman at Columbia University, I received a call from a producer of MTV's reality television show *True Life*, which highlighted issues affecting adolescents and young adults (sexuality, relationships, addiction, depression, etc.). I had reached out first by answering an ad on an eating disorders support website looking for people willing to participate in a short documentary. My motivation for doing so was multifaceted, but essentially boiled down to my hope that maybe if I *proved* my anorexia (to myself and to others), I could accept it as real and let it go. I was seduced by the prospect of telling my story. This was a familiar endeavor for me, the pursuit of some ephemeral legitimizing factor, clutching at moments that presented the possibility of validation, which always faded or were negated in the end. (It would take me many years after that to realize that all this was an intellectual, highly sophisticated ruse on the part of my anorexia to procrastinate beginning the healing process, to get me to lose *just one more pound*.)

The producer and I spoke a number of times. She was interested in my current plight, which was that the staff at Schneider Children's Hospital, a division of Long Island Jewish, was considering transferring me to another hospital or kicking me out of the program because I wasn't gaining any weight. (Oh, the suspense. Will she pull it together? Will she eat her hard-boiled eggs? Will she *survive?*) Finally, the producer told me she wanted to send a cameraperson to film me while I went about my daily activities. I panicked. My first thought: *they are going see that you look totally normal, fat, even, and turn the car around. You won't compare to the other subjects, all bony, perfect for the angle-loving eyes of a camera. They'll curse a day of lost filming.* My second thought: *my parents will be so humiliated to have my eating disorder broadcast to an entire nation.* My parents are not overly secretive or repressed people, but they are Puritan in that they don't like the idea of airing your dirty laundry. I had always been terrified of embarrassing them—these perfect, wedding-cake people with wholesome hobbies and photo albums organized chronologically. I was doing just that—embarrassing them—by being sick in the first place, but to reveal my dull, tortured life like that on TV would be worse than humiliating: it would be *trashy.*

So I stopped responding to the producer's phone calls. I planned to call her office in the middle of the night when I knew she wouldn't answer so I could leave an explanatory message, but I never did. The episode aired a few months later when I was an inpatient at Cornell, and I remember being exceedingly glad I didn't have access to cable television. Of course, a large portion was filmed at the media-friendly Renfrew Center. I heard the Cornell staff chatting about it and mocking one of the participants, a former Cornell patient named Veronica. I mentioned her to my friend later that night.

"You know Veronica Hagen?" my friend said. "She's been everywhere. She's, like, toured the country from hospital to hospital."

No, I didn't know Veronica, I said. I just knew she was on TV.

My interpretation of my reaction to my would-be television debut has changed over the years. At the time, I felt a pang of regret for how I handled it. Mostly I was disappointed in myself for dealing with the situation in such a passive-aggressive way. As time progressed, as I relapsed and got well, went into remission, relapsed, and got well again, I became increasingly confident in my belief that appearing on the show would have been somewhere between insignificant and actually detrimental to my recovery. To have this souvenir of my sickest days? This wouldn't be just a memento, but a piece in a medium that would allow me, in an Aristotelian way, to reexperience the tragedy of my illness, a CD I could pop in my DVD player and curl up on the couch and be lulled to sleep by. I again invoke my favorite analogy for eating disorders: abusive lovers. And what do you do when someone is in an abusive relationship? You don't allow visitation rights, weekly dates. You don't put them in the vicinity of or let the abuser flirt with them. You *keep them the fuck away.*

Back to the first demographic of those interested in *Thin*: the bystanders, the parents and loved ones. They are trickier. For them it's not an issue of seduction (and therefore not as immediately, or perhaps directly, destructive), but in reality, texts of this nature can be classified as something like a social pollutant.

One very cold autumn evening, my college friend Marisa and I were wandering around a bookstore on Saint Mark's Place in the East Village of New York City. The independent store was stocked with tiny 'zines and avant-garde magazines in addition to the typical art books and fiction and nonfiction titles. As I flipped through a copy of a book by Colette, I noticed that Marisa was standing at the middle display table slowly turning the pages of *Thin*, transfixed, mouth slightly gaped. I hustled away. I knew what *Thin* was. I had written a convoluted letter of protest to *People* magazine denouncing it after they excerpted it in an article (the letter was never published). I had heard the angry ripples throughout the tri-state eating disorders community. People went to therapy weeping because they didn't look like Alisa or Amanda or Suzy Carrot Sticks. Girls nearly recovered morbidly imagined what they *would* have done had they seen Rachel's meal plan when they had been sick. My therapist told me I wasn't the only patient to enter her office brandishing the issue of *People* in a clenched fist.

Had *Thin* been available when I was younger, it might have been a different story, but at this point in my life, I worked hard to stay far away from anything I thought might trigger any internal anorexic comparison. I resisted my dirty interest in seeing it, and lingered in the back hoping that Marisa would move on to another book and I wouldn't have to get too close and risk glimpsing an image that might spark a pang of jealousy. When I meandered toward the front of the store sometime later, she was still leaning over the big glossy book, so I decided to interrupt her, mainly to try to pull her away so we could leave the store, but ulterior motives could have been involved (they usually are).

When I walked up beside her, she was quiet for a few seconds. Then she said, "So horrible. Can you believe people have to see things like this?"

Now, I'll try really hard not to push the obvious caveat *(I'm not saying I am now or ever was as "good" or sick as any of the subjects of* Thin), but clinically, I was at times some type of horrible, or at least was temporarily housed in facilities where people were as good/sick as the patients profiled in *Thin* (more so, maybe), facilities that Marisa had seen when she came to visit me. My first reaction was irritation born of that pesky anorexic inferiority complex. *She doesn't think I was ever really sick. Which, of course, must mean I wasn't.*

But wait a minute, I thought later . . . Marisa had grasped the severity at times. After all, this is the girl who, outside a bar one night, confided in me that she had often told herself, *If Kelsey dies tonight, I guess I will just kill myself.* This was the friend who wrote to me years later of times when I was ill, "I didn't know if you were going to make it out okay, in all honesty." She was there when a tiny bone in my foot snapped as I was walking down the stairs one morning our senior year of college, and she was there when I came home with a portable ultrasound machine designed to stimulate bone growth because the stubborn metatarsal refused to heal for months afterward. She knew, as much as one could, the impact that this disease had on my life and the lives of my family. So maybe it wasn't about me, but rather about *presentation*. Maybe her reaction supported Ludwig Andreas Feuerbach's analysis of modernity as a time in which society "prefers the sign to the thing signified, the copy to the original, representation to reality, the appearance to the essence . . . Illusion only is sacred, truth profane. Nay, sacredness is held to be enhanced in proportion as truth decreases and illusion increases, so that the highest degree of

illusion comes to be the highest degree of sacredness."
Maybe there was just something more immediate and potent
and accessible about the large-scale pictures of the emaciated
elderly woman tracing her figure on a big piece of construction paper, the chubby girl with the mascara-stained face and
naked limbs splayed out to display lines and lines of scars. (I
kept mine hidden, for the most part.)

"There was natural drama and tension that was emotional, narrative, and cinematic," Greenfield writes in her
introduction.

Beauty, regularity, and form: the seduction of the story.

Drama and tension are there in droves, but it can't be
considered "natural" if you choose your subjects, pose
them, adjust the lighting, edit the material, and print on
glossy nine-by-twelve sheets of paper or splice the film in an
editing room. In real time, even the sickest narratives lack
that "cinematic" quality, because there are days of imperceptible tweaks to diet and fumbled, senseless actions that
would inevitably have a workshop class member questioning the "point" of such an act.

"I just don't think it's in line with her *chaaaaa-racter,*"
a critic would say while underlining a section of the text he
feels "doesn't belong," a scene in which the spindly protagonist commits an act that, in some way, does not fit the plot.

So I think for these people, the loved ones, a book like
Thin makes it possible to harbor the delusion that *this* is
what an eating-disordered person looks like, not my friend
next to me who sometimes eats a peanut butter and jelly
sandwich (and then frantically runs up and down flights of

stairs and swallows a box of laxative pills offstage right, or doesn't, either way). *Real* anorexics are on *Oprah* and never crack. *Real* anorexics look like her, bounce in and out of hospitals. *Real* anorexics have feeding tubes, exhibit all the symptoms listed in the *DSM*. *Thin* offers the illusion that there is a narrative there, some A, B, C that is often a mirage. It offers stock characters against which family members and friends can compare the real people closest to them.

Well, at least you weren't as sick as she was.

Which, I hope by now you realize, is one of the worst things you could say to an anorexic.

Well, I'll get there. I'll show them.

CHAPTER 8

PLATEAU/CLIMAX

AROUND THE TIME I FIRST STARTED SPEAKING WITH THE MTV producer, my therapist at Schneider Children's Hospital was trying to get me to maintain my weight. This wasn't their normal practice with day program patients, she told me; most were encouraged to gain more than a pound a week, but I had been there for over a week, sitting around in groups making collages with high schoolers, and mine was dropping. The doctors performed all sorts of medical tests—EKGs and metabolism rate analyses on top of the standard vital checks—and discovered that my body was, to put it generously, totally fucked. When I managed over one night to stay the exact same weight, my therapist wasn't impressed.

"With your metabolism as slow as it is, you could eat nothing and maintain your weight."

When I arrived at Schneider, I was raw from a bout that had begun with an offhand comment from my boyfriend concerning my hip bones. ("Stop sucking in," he had admonished.) It wasn't his fault, but sometimes that's all it takes: a comment, a stray glance, an Adderall a friend gives you so you can sit down and just *focus* on a paper. A few days of minor deprivation, that certain jumpiness, and my brain just clicked. A familiar companion, back again after two years of lying dormant.

Remember me?

At first, the relapse felt rote, or normal. When I entered college, I considered myself to be a recovered anorexic— past tense—and when I began to fall back into old habits, I figured I would eventually cave and give in to the pleasures of collegiate life. I believed, as so many "recovered" anorexics I've met do, that I would never have the kind of willpower to starve again. It soon became clear, though, that I was very wrong. My behavior and my appearance deteriorated, and suddenly everyone knew that there was something wrong with me. One night, I sat in the stairwell in my dorm talking to my boyfriend on the phone, and he told me that a high school classmate of mine had drunkenly scoffed when my name was mentioned at a party.

"Kelsey's so bad, she's *so anorexic*," the girl had slurred.

"She said that?" was my response.

He was too sweet to say it in an accusatory manner, but he did point out that my tone of voice, over the phone, had a tinge of smugness to it. He was right, and I knew it.

What he didn't understand, or at least I assume he didn't, was that I didn't care if people thought I was crazy. The key was that if she had called me *anorexic,* then she was automatically implying that I was thin, and that's what I worked so hard for every single minute of every single day.

Poor boyfriend, whom I had started dating during a time of remission in high school, had watched me go from a relatively normal college freshman into a totally self-obsessed, cold little creature, alien and jumpy and angry. Even though some part of me knew I didn't want *him* specifically anymore, or anyone, in fact—that I couldn't handle a relationship other than the one I had with Ziploc bags and green apples—I kept him around, so selfish was I in my desire to get some quick comfort in times of need. He was naive and thought he could love me toward health, and I was ruthless and manipulative, calling him, weepy and plaintive, when I felt particularly on edge, and shunning his attention when I wanted to be alone. Thanksgiving break, when I visited him at his house, I curled up beneath his heated blanket in front of a space heater and refused to be cuddled, instead preferring to fall asleep bathed in simulated warmth, like a premature chick in an incubator.

By the time I left school for Christmas break, I was desperately afraid for my life. I believed I could *feel* my mental faculties atrophying, and often found myself telling bemused dorm neighbors, "I think I'm going crazy." I got frequent headaches and it became difficult to read, and so I put on gigantic headphones and bundled myself up in depressing music and slept or walked around campus aimlessly. Sometimes I ventured farther afield and wandered random city streets; once I ended up nearly in tears in the middle of Grand Central, where I had gone perhaps because it was a place that reminded me of being young and holding my father's hand. I hid in the stairwells of my college dormitory after running the twelve flights bottom to top and slammed my head into the concrete wall. I frequently blacked out sitting in my chair during class and "woke up" to realize that twenty, thirty minutes had passed. On occasion, I shit blood. I hadn't expected to get so sick, to feel so consistently physically awful. I had begun this particular anorexic quest in a routinely sentimental, dramatic fashion and ended it with a detachment the likes of which I couldn't fathom until months afterward, at which point I could only react by crying and, against my better judgment, praying. I listened to Cat Stevens's "Trouble" on repeat, clasped my hands together, waited for the piano's entrance, and focused all my feeble energy on begging the universe for respite.

One could make the argument that I don't really understand it even now, almost a decade later. What would it mean to do that, to understand? Embrace the girl who runs up and down the myriad flights of stairs in her dorm building, who pours a spoonful of yogurt into the sink to ensure that she won't consume all the calories contained within the cup? In some way comprehend the child who lambastes herself for not having the courage to throw her sick little body from her third-floor hospital window?

No, I do not want to know that girl. She was feeble, sad, and boring.

When my father brought me to Schneider Children's Hospital for my initial evaluation, I told the doctor, a clammy old man with a walleye, that I wanted to enroll in the day program and that I was motivated to get better. He looked at me askance, but I was so slow on the uptake that it hardly registered. I didn't *think* I was lying; I thought if I had some structure in place, I could take care of the rest, even though being an outpatient hadn't worked when I was at Silver Hill. This time would be different. This time I would try really, really hard.

The doctor took me to an exam room and asked me to put on a gown. Then he left me sitting there on the cold plastic bench for what seemed like an hour. I heard the ruckus of children outside the door and felt tears falling onto my cheeks. I kept asking in my head repeatedly, *Why have you left me alone here?* When he came back, he had a medical student in tow, and he directed all his comments about me to her.

"She has no reflexes in her feet whatsoever. Do you see?" He knocked them with the little rubber hammer once again, but my toes stayed still as a cadaver's.

"Is that because of the sickness?" I said, but he didn't answer.

Right before I left with instructions to return for breakfast the next day, the doctor looked at me sideways again and asked me about a doctor I had been seeing at university health services.

"And Dr. Atkin didn't think you needed to go inpatient?" he asked.

"She didn't think my weight was low enough."

I didn't catch it at the time, but he had wanted to put me inpatient. "He wanted to give you *the tube,*" my therapist told me. When I learned that, I regretted that I hadn't made my distress clearer during my initial interview. I have never been one to really lay my emotions bare, and even in the direst of psychiatric states, I have been described as poised and articulate. I wished that I had screamed and clawed at myself or told them of how the night before my evaluation, I had lied and said I was eating with my boyfriend, but instead I sat alone in my car in the parking lot of a Stop & Shop and ate a yogurt before downing a box of laxatives. After that, I had gone to babysit, and when the kids were asleep, I called my boyfriend and unceremoniously told him that I wanted to break up, then waited impatiently as he worked through his emotions. Severing one of my strongest ties with my healthy self felt simply like a relief.

I wished that they had just made the decision to put me inpatient immediately and taken away my free nights, which I filled with push-ups and trips to CVS to buy more laxatives. But they hadn't, and so there I was, at my crossroads. On Friday, my therapist asked me if there were any foods I would be comfortable eating over the weekend.

"Eggs? Milk?"

I thought she was kind of an airhead, with her streaked hair and her nasally Long Island accent, but her hopefulness was touching, and so I nodded my head yes to eggs. She grinned and wrote down "hard-boiled eggs" on an index card. But the weekend came and went and I never ate them, and on Monday, every medical test that was performed on me again came back with dismal results. My blood pressure was erratic, my metabolism the speed of someone comatose. My therapist had confided in me that during rounds, another staff member said she was afraid I would keel over from a heart attack at any moment. When they weighed me, I saw that the number had dropped and I knew there would be consequences. I looked up at my therapist and asked her what was going to happen.

"I'll have to discuss it with the staff," she said.

Normally a patient who didn't comply with the program at Schneider's would be shipped off to a psychiatric hospital, usually Cornell, or tossed out, but the staff decided instead to have me admitted as an inpatient there at Long Island Jewish so that I could be medically monitored. When I heard the ruling, I burst into tears, but I agreed to it. Over the course of that day, I repeatedly pestered the tech (basically the ward babysitter—like a nurse without the degree) to tell me if the admission was a plot on the part of the doctors to make me believe I was worse (or, to me and my compatriots, better) than I actually was, a grand scheme to rob my parents' insurance company. If that was the case, I would insist that they give a more deserving child the bed and just let me die, though I doubted I had the force of will to starve to death. The tech, Becky, a sweet young Asian woman who shepherded the flock of patients from the main hospital building to the day treatment center and back again, asked me if I knew what my blood pressure was. I told her what the doctor had told me that morning.

"That's, like, heart attack."

I remained unconvinced, but on New Year's Eve 2002, I placed piles of clothes in little hospital drawers, signed a "Do not resuscitate" order, and shuffled over to an exam room to have an IV inserted. When the doctor poked my hand with the needle, my blood pressure crashed, my head floated up toward the ceiling, and two nurses led me by my elbows to bed. I rose two hours later to watch the ball drop. The nurses cheered and gave the other patient and me glasses of apple juice. I left mine untouched on the plastic table.

Despite the above lip service to my eating disorder, I didn't *appear* that ill, even carting around that IV pole my first few days. My insides were in terrible shape, but my outsides could pass for "a little too thin." Celebrity thin, not thirty-five-pound-wonder-on-the-Dr.-Phil-show thin. Even my doctor at Columbia, who examined me once a week and had recognized my cardiac irregularities, told me she didn't think my weight was low enough for me to be hospitalized. Of course, I thought this meant I was fat, and this simple fact would override any frequent chest pains I was having and render me unworthy of treatment or attention or food or *anything*. But this doctor, I think even now, was lacking in intuition on many levels. Most trained eyes (usually those belonging to eating-disordered individuals) could have spotted the telltale signs of my starvation: the hunched shoulders and cracked red knuckles, the unusually thick hair that covered my arms in a last-ditch effort to keep me warm, the bags under the eyes that were etched just slightly too deep.

As Jackie said, "Anorexics don't always look too thin. They just look *wrong*."

It was here at Schneider Children's that I met Orah. Orah looked wrong. For starters, she looked maybe eight years old even though she was actually twelve. When she was admitted, I had already been there a week or so. I was already sharper than I had been during my evaluation, when it had taken me five minutes or so to really *understand* what people were saying to me, as if they were speaking in code and I had to decipher it silently before I could respond.

I first saw Orah standing in the unit's tiny hallway, facing the wall and weeping quietly. She was right outside my room, number 327, by an abandoned cot. The cot, which was empty because a room had freed up, is an image that weighs heavily in my memory; it is the one in which a patient slept when I first arrived, a patient of indeterminate sex and dark skin who writhed and groaned all throughout the morning, whose twisted visage was ignored by the passing doctors and nurses and hospital personnel.

Orah's knuckles were in far worse shape than mine, the dehydrated, pink, flaking skin in stark contrast to the rest of her alabaster body. Her eyes were huge and open too wide, her mouth slightly agape, and she wouldn't sit down unless instructed to. The other patients, myself included, stared at her. We ceased playing our little mealtime games: the prestidigitations involving forks and napkins, the analysis of one patient's plate, then the next, to determine who was consuming what (vegetable, carbohydrate, protein) and at what speed, the position shifting and shaking of feet beneath the table and other cheap attempts at clandestine exercise.

"Shall we do patient orientation?" someone asked.

"Orah's been here before," said Marlene, the lumbering Caribbean nurse.

It seemed there was no need to inform Orah of the rules of the dining room. She was aware not only of the rules particular to Schneider's, but to those of other institutions as well. We spent the next forty-five minutes, our allotted mealtime, asking her questions in soft, cautious tones, listening to her answer in a babyish whisper about her stay at LIJ and Cornell, about her OCD, about running up and down the stairs in her family's Brooklyn home, stopping at a predetermined spot on the linoleum floor to cry. Our heads dropped ever so slightly as if we were all trying to meet her gaze.

"After this, I will either go back to Cornell or go home."

"Who will decide?"

"Dr. Silver."

She disappeared after dinner and returned wearing a large T-shirt, an IV pole trailing behind her. Her figure was dwarfed by her metal companion and made her seem that much more fragile and loveable. When she retreated to her room, I followed her and found her circling her bed aimlessly.

"Hi," I offered.

"Hi." She plopped down on the cot and I followed her lead. There we remained for the next two hours.

I learned a lot about her that evening. I learned that her mother had died when she was five, that her father was a doctor. She told me how many Cheerios she had eaten the first day of her first admission and how at Cornell, which she called Westchester, she had often been reprimanded for throwing her little body into walls, which she did to protest when they wouldn't let her outside to play. I told her about myself, too, about my current struggles with body image. I didn't tell her about when I stood on my toes to try to view my entire torso in the small bathroom mirror, nor did I stress my despondency over weight gain, my retreat beneath my meager bedsheet after morning weigh-in, and the seemingly endless flow of tears that followed. She was so young, and I didn't want to expose her to anything I felt would be inappropriate.

But I did tell her what I weighed.

"That's really low!" she exclaimed. I rushed to deny it. *I'm short. It just sounds low. Don't get the wrong impression. I'm not so bad off. Such a "good" anorexic.*

"I don't know. For me, it was never really about body image," she said. "It's just . . . I was always the smallest in my class, and I just wanted to stay that way. To stay small."

I told Orah about my first EKG at the hospital, my strange heartbeat, what the fish-eyed doctor had called a *junctional rhythm*. My brain was telling my heart to beat, and the heart wasn't responding quickly enough, or something like that. I hadn't been able to listen. When I was first admitted, I had been given what they call telemetry, which is a portable heart-monitoring device about the size and shape of an iPod. All the eating-disordered patients were, in fact, hooked up to telemetry. The little box was connected by wires to six round stickies that were placed strategically on your chest and belly. They itched like hell, but you could only remove them when you were in the shower, where you could claw at the little red circles they left on your skin until they turned raw and bled. These red circles, chapped with flecks of congealed blood once you were dry, acted as miniature targets so you could reattach the next batch. The telemetry readings were monitored on a screen in the back of the nurses' station. Sometimes we would peer behind the desk to see our little mountain ranges.

"Show me mine!" Orah once asked.

"And mine!" I echoed, thinking that maybe if I saw my own heartbeat I would finally understand something about being in a body, about being human.

My cardiac anomalies (discharge papers read: bradycardia, orthostatics, junctional rhythm) were the principle reasons why, ultimately, they decided to have me admitted to Adolescent Medicine as opposed to shipping me off to Cornell or another strictly psychiatric facility. They wanted to monitor my heart with telemetry and do a few more tests because they had seen a few odd blips that raised eyebrows. First, they did an echocardiogram, which is essentially a sonogram of the heart. As I lay on the exam table, watching the grainy pulsating picture of my heart on the screen, I could think of little more than my rock-hard, distended stomach and how humiliating it was that the sweet nurse had to see it naked and protruding like that. After that, a few people from the cardiology unit came to see me. They hooked me up to what they called a Holter monitor, a device a bit bigger than the telemetry that was kept in a black fanny pack that snapped around my waist. Now I had twice as many stickies attached to my torso. Twice as many stickies, twice as many pockmarks. The readings from this monitor would be evaluated by a cardiologist, and after twenty-four hours, they would come back and tell me what they found. When they did, they reported that all was well.

"What about the junctional rhythm?" I asked.

"We didn't see any evidence of a junctional rhythm," the woman replied.

I was disappointed. Maybe if that box had been checked off, I would have felt complete, real, a "good enough" anorexic?

You must have made it up, came the snarl, *to get attention, to be admitted. What kind of an anorexic would do that? A fake one. What kind of person? A parasite.*

"We tell ourselves stories in order to live," Joan Didion writes in "The White Album," an essay exploring narrative and the Self, capitalized.

Here is a story my former psychiatrist tells herself, and me, the myth that allows her to see me as a typical acute anorexic and herself as the token medical professional who contributed to said's recovery process. Lynn Redgrave, maybe, in the film version of *Girl, Interrupted*.

Referring to what some might call my most serious bout with anorexia, my first semester of my freshman year in college leading up to my admission at Schneider's, she says, "I remember when I first met you, you had lanugo on your face. Do you remember that?" She nods and stares at me with a distant, authoritative maternal expression, one typical of women in health care. Clad in black nylons, she recrosses her legs and unfolds her hands and raises them toward her cheeks and strokes them. "You had soft white hair on your face, almost like a beard. You had facial hair!" She laughs with disgusted joy, as if to say, *Thank God you aren't like that anymore!*

"Do you remember?" she asks again.

I say yes, but I don't remember. I remember being evaluated at Schneider's, the doctor asking me if the hair on my arms was a "normal amount," plumage I had been endowed with by nature. I said, "I guess not," though I didn't know then, either. I couldn't tell. He moved the flap of my gown aside to show the student doctor my upper back, used the same phrase, "soft white hair," but maybe that was normal, too, or maybe it wasn't. I didn't know. I couldn't see it. It seemed a lot when I was cold and it stood up on its ends, but it always had . . . hadn't it? I was so often cold.

But it was winter.

My psychiatrist has had this conversation with me numerous times. Each time I say yes, I remember, I remember the lanugo. I invest my words in the myth of my anorexia, its severity, in order to live, literally. Each time, I search my memory for other indications that this period of time during which I had "soft white hair" on my face really did exist, but I come up blank. No one else with whom I was close has ever mentioned it. I turn the memory over and over again in my hands, like a smooth river stone. I think about all the memories in close proximity to it, my anorexia itself. I take a little behavioral walk into the past to try to re-create it, but it remains the unlaid ghost, and I am beginning to think it will never be understood, and I will have to live with this.

• • •

FOR A GOOD DEAL OF TIME EVEN AFTER I HAD A FIRM "RECOVery" foundation, I convinced myself that I was cruelly exaggerating the seriousness of my eating disorder in order to have a story to tell. I was never really *that bad*. I never weighed as little as Marya Hornbacher. I never had a feeding tube. I was in the hospital *this* many times, not *that* many. I even constructed this brilliant, albeit twisted, argument that I had *never* had an eating disorder at all; that at heights of starvation, I had been living a lifestyle that suited me, that was somehow right for my physical and emotional constitution, yet I was so desperate for attention that I had conned doctors into giving me the label I so transparently wanted in hopes that it would placate the actress in me and, in turn, let me take a back door to justifying all sorts of future self-indulgence (i.e., eating junk food and eschewing exercise, among other things). I imagined the doctors snickering to one another during rounds as they doodled on my charts. "Let her have her *experience*. I just feel bad for her insurance provider."

I realize now that the nonexistence of my eating disorder is sort of a hard sell. It looks pretty real on paper. Number of hospitalizations over how many years. Symptoms exhibited. Bone density at ages eighteen, twenty-one, twenty-four. Blood pressure Thanksgiving of 2002, 2003,

2004. Compile my anorexic résumé and no sane individual would give any merit to my claims of "fake" or "less than" anorexic status. So I think, *Maybe this is a good plan.* Maybe I should get all the information together, write a blow-by-blow narrative, make it something I can *touch* and therefore not *deny*, and finally lay it to rest.

I started this process in March of 2007 by looking into my medical records from hospitalization number two, at Schneider's in January of 2003. It was during this hospitalization that a doctor had told me I was close to being considered "chronic." What that meant in the grand scheme of things I didn't really know, but it sounded serious. I had seen that discharge sheet. "Bradycardia, orthostatics, osteopenia." All those medical terms sounded so official and comforting. There were bound to be pages upon pages of them.

I researched how to get my records from Schneider's. The hospital required that you give them a signed request in writing along with some identifying facts.

"Will my records still be there if I was there a few years ago? I mean, how long do you guys keep the records?" I asked the man who answered the phone.

"When were you here?"

"Four years ago—2003."

"Oh, yeah, definitely." His certainty bordered on joy. "We keep records for up to ten years. We just move them to an off-site location in Queens."

I thought of my records shivering like poorly clad orphans in a drafty Queens warehouse. They were indistinguishable from all the other stacks of paper surrounding them, yet they were my facts in there, my story. They belonged to no one but me. I began to think of my medical records as my tiny, neglected children whom I had to rescue.

About a week and a half after I had sent in my paperwork, my mother called me to ask about a letter she had received.

"Kelsey, did you request your medical records from LIJ?"

"Yes."

"Is everything okay?"

My first reaction was chagrined. Why must every reference to my past be bad? Can't we recognize that sometimes we'll all have to think about it?

"It's for research."

"Okay, well, this letter says it's going to cost you $127.65."

I wondered how long my records were, thinking for a moment that the longer the records, the more significant my story. To copy one page at the Kinko's down my street cost fourteen cents a page. $127.65 divided by .14 equals 911 pages. Just a hair shorter than my edition of *Ulysses*. My story was an epic.

I decided I wasn't going to request them, partly because it aroused suspicion and partly because I didn't have the money. I also wondered if maybe there were things in there that I shouldn't know, and that even *owning* this document, carving a spot for the monolith in the corner of my bedroom, might accomplish the exact opposite of what I wanted it to. Instead of letting it go, I'd be reminded of it constantly. I would sift through the pages and be *close* to it again, more inclined to let it take up my time, my life. I could read it like a novel, wade among all the happy diagnoses, but I suspected eventually it wouldn't be enough to know I once had them; I would have to *have* them, present tense. Nostalgia only goes so far.

Two months later, I received a call from a Ronitte De-Silva.

"Hello, Kelsey, this is Ronitte DeSilva from Schneider Children's Hospital at LIJ. I'm just calling regarding your medical records. We pulled them nine weeks ago, so I'm calling to see if you still want them. Give me a call back."

Nine. Every time I listened to my message, the robotic voice would inform me that I had "one . . . saved . . . message" and I would let her know by pressing "9" that I wanted to save it for another twenty-one days. *I'm not ready yet, so stop bothering me,* I'd think. *I still haven't decided.*

Cliffhanger.

• • •

ORAH'S SPIRIT LIGHTENED QUICKLY. SOON, SHE WAS AN EAGER sprite with a wry, commercial-worthy smile, one that lifted to the side of her face and was accompanied by a raising of her eyebrows. She and another patient and I worked tirelessly on a three-dimensional train puzzle and then left it atop the metal closets for all to behold. We mined any opportunity for humor or unadulterated enjoyment. Gary, the dayroom attendant, firmly believed in the healing power of music, and one morning he shut the door and had all fifteen eating-disordered patients sit in a circle with different instruments and we jammed, banging haphazardly on cheap plastic bongos, shaking a mallet of bells. Our voices lifted up and melted into one another despite their atonality, and Orah's hands clapped with a child's nascent sense of rhythm. Indeed, I liked to think of her as my child, in a way. She didn't have a mother, and she was so small. I stayed close by her at all times, as if I believed that my mere presence would protect her from the noxious social air of the unit. I didn't want her to have to listen to the other patients' constant storytelling: ruptured esophagi and failed interventions and stretchers, tricks and games and lies told with smiles. I didn't know what I thought I was protecting her from, though. She knew that world already, maybe better than I did. I watched her pop pill after pill without the aid of water.

"This one is Lexapro, and this one . . ."

One evening, I went to my room before dinner to find that I had a new roommate. Her name was Mariah and she was a twelve-year-old ballet dancer from Manhattan. She was branchy bodied, with a high, squeaky voice, still-lustrous brown hair flecked with spots of gold, and limbs covered in downy lanugo. She looked like a fuzzy alien, a creature from the planet Emaciated. She was a hospital neophyte and pled vegetarianism at her first meal, while the rest of us rolled our eyes at one another, knowing that she'd eat that chicken sooner or later. We fixated on her and her little arms. Patients would ask her to sit on their laps and then make faces of shock and mouth "tailbone" while she giggled and colored in the book on the table in front of her. Her doctor sent her for an MRI to see if her anorexia had shrunk her brain, and she returned to the lounge afterward with a Band-Aid–shaped spot of clean, hairless skin smack in the middle of her furry forehead. When my father saw her one day while visiting me and learned how old she was, he said, "Wow. She got good *fast*."

So other people see this as strength, too, I thought. *Something to be good at.*

While I was reading in the dayroom one Sunday afternoon, Orah walked up to me, her eyes cast downward. She stood silently in front of my chair until I spoke.

"What's wrong?"

"Mariah's so skinny," she whispered.

Before there had been no one to compare herself to, no template against which she could measure her illness.

"But Mariah's twelve like me," she said.

"Do you want to look like her?" I asked her, though I knew the answer.

"I don't know." Her voice was barely audible even in the empty room, her prepubescent lexicon not developed enough to do justice to the iniquity of what rumbled in her mind right then. "I think when I go home, maybe, I would want to try and get skinny like her."

"I know how hard it is when you compare yourself to those around you, I really do. But you have to remember that she is very sick, and this isn't the way she's going to look forever. She'll have to get to her target weight eventually, too. You don't want to live like this. I look around at everyone else here, everyone"—I stressed this because even I looked at twelve-year-old Mariah in her toddler's hospital gown (she didn't even fit into the regular kids' ones) and swooned at the sight of her toothpick legs—"and wish I looked like them. But we have to be strong and remember that this is part of why we fight. We have to fight to be well, fight against this thing that tells us we need to look sick to be happy. Do you want to be happy and go home and play football?" Despite her small stature, she was a big football and basketball fan.

"Yes."

"I know you do. You just have to keep fighting. I know it's hard. You just have to be strong."

"Okay," she whimpered.

We hugged. I made her promise to get in touch with me whenever she needed anything, no matter where she was. I would protect her. I would take care of her.

My speech was heartfelt, but my mind was duplicitous. The rules of love and shelter and food applied to Orah but not to me. That evening at dinner she, Mariah, the two other patients, and I all stood at the table with our plates in front of us. I looked at my tray: the bread, the chicken, the little packet of butter. Windows of opportunity were opening and closing. I didn't want that stupid packet of butter; I didn't *need* that packet of butter. When Marlene turned around, I lifted it from the tray and stuck it on a little ledge beneath the table.

You've got some fancy moves with your napkin, young lady, a voice from the past chastised me in my head. I had always been very quick with my hands, a veritable magician. Now you see it, now you don't.

Just as I was congratulating myself, convincing myself that it was no big deal—like the leg lifts I did in my bed, like the sneaking of diet beverages from the hospital gift store— the supervising nurse walked in.

"She had a packet of butter," Marlene said to the nurse, looking at me. "Where did your butter go?"

"I didn't see any," I said.

"I saw it. I know it was there. Where is it?"

"I don't know what you're talking about. I didn't see anything."

They made me empty my pockets, to no avail. I wasn't too worried, because I knew they wouldn't find it.

"I don't know what you did with it, but it was there."

I considered myself triumphant until I looked at Orah, all marble-eyed innocent. It was perhaps the first moment in my life as an anorexic, looking at this tiny creature I felt so maternal toward, that I considered the possibility that I was enabling a legacy of illness.

Orah was discharged from Schneider's a few days after the butter incident. She went home, but—spoiler alert—we would meet again at Cornell some four months later. I had been there for three weeks when a nurse asked me if I knew Orah.

"Why do you ask?"

"She's coming for a readmission."

My heart wilted. She hadn't made it. Flipping through a unit coloring book a while earlier, I had noticed a page with her name written in large letters in crayon in the bottom right-hand corner; the picture was half finished. Now she would be able to complete it.

"Why? What happened?" I fired off questions to no avail.

"Sometimes people need a readmission." Janine shrugged.

I waited all day, until finally after dinner the door opened and there she was, marching onto the unit like a teeny somnambulist, her father trailing close behind her. She wore the same blank-cum-sad expression she had when first admitted to LIJ, and so I put myself in her path and waited for the recognition to hit. When it did, her face changed and grew a charming little smile. She came bolting down the hallway, and I picked her up and spun her around. It is one image in a series of memories from Cornell that rise to the surface now, flashes of: her fainting in the hallway, her little limbs going stiff and her body toppling over, my rush to hide my teary face in a friend's shoulder; her dancing oh-so-slowly with another patient to Al Green one warm spring day; the hospital name game we played my last night as an inpatient, my mouth's sour taste after rattling off mutual acquaintances; her lament to my mother when she arrived to take me home.

"I don't want Kelsey to leave."

"Well, you get out of here and you two can see each other at home. Neither one of you are allowed to come back here ever again."

Once Orah was discharged from Cornell, I went to see

her march in the Israel Day Parade on Fifth Avenue on a rainy summer day in 2003. A few months later, I visited her in Brooklyn and went to her grandmother's house for Shabbat lunch. I was clearly the outsider, the blonde with the nose ring and white wool cocoon coat confronted with a table of gefilte fish and cholent, but I was tolerated. I stayed and played football with her and snapped her picture for my photography class. She stood on the two-foot-high fence around the porch of her family's modest Brooklyn home and turned back to face me.

"It's like the last look back before jumping off a ledge," my teacher said about the photo in class, and I dropped my head so he couldn't see my eyes well up with tears.

Orah got sick again and then better again. We fell out of touch, though occasionally I would get a brief e-mail from her asking if I remembered the time we played ball in her yard and I ruined my shoes. I wasn't surprised that we had grown apart. What had brought us together, after all, was our diagnosis, and our bond was based on something appropriately thin and brittle. It is difficult to remain close to people you meet in rehab despite the deep stirrings you feel with them when you're there; to know their medical histories and emotional paroxysms before such banalities as where they went to school or what street they live on is almost like trying to build a house from the roof down. Orah and I also came from radically different worlds that happened to be geographically close. I was a college student in Manhattan, originally from a notoriously WASPy enclave in Connecticut, and she came from a tight-knit, even more insular Orthodox community in Brooklyn. (Schneider's, in fact, is where my obsession with Orthodox Jews, another community of "special" people to which I never felt I could really belong, was born. There were a great many there, and I have spent much time over the ensuing years theorizing as to why these youngsters would be a particularly at-risk population.)

After a few years of sparse communication, I received an unexpected e-mail from Orah. She was eighteen, no longer the child I had known but a young woman, about to travel halfway around the world to spend the year at a yeshiva in Jerusalem. I was struck by how funny she was, the effervescence of her brief sentences. She told me she was my height. We made plans to meet for tea somewhere in between our homes, and I found myself quite pensive in the days leading up to it. Would she still feel like my fey little girl, a delicate flower I must shield from the rain? Or would her voice and limbs be full of fortitude and self-assurance? And if she had rosy cheeks, would that mean that it was really over, that the past was gone and my anorexia, something I never believed was real in the first place, was now dead?

And would that make me happy or sad?

CHAPTER 9

HOSPITALS

At Schneider's, I also met a girl named Jenna Rabinowitz. Jenna was fat; not obese, but certainly overweight. She was consistently clad in sweatpants and a long-sleeved cotton field hockey T-shirt, a Long Island teenager uniform of sorts. Around her wrist were five ID bracelets from various ER visits and hospital admissions. She explained that she kept them on so she "would remember." It was an aposiopesis of sorts; we were supposed to fill in the ending, but I, and probably a number of the other girls, knew that this was not the purpose these bracelets served. They were badges of honor, meant to remind her, and all of us, of how valiant a fighter she was. When she spoke of them, it wasn't with sadness or regret or even with a hint of fear. She raised her chin and stiffened her shoulders when she told us of ambulance rides and seventy-two-hour admissions. She was proud.

Jenna had recently been discharged from Cornell Westchester and had come to the Schneider's day program for aftercare. She wasted no time in regaling us with stories of this legendary institution. Cornell was where my friend Lisa had been hospitalized years earlier, where I would land just four months after leaving Schneider's and again two years later, when I would meet Lily, the famous New York City anorexic who wore her feeding tube to school.

I knew Cornell because it was relatively close to my house. The estate-esque grounds were hidden from the busy road and highway that bordered them by a fence and a thick padding of trees, endowing it with a sense of impenetrability. It seemed the very definition of "insane asylum," Ivy League brick buildings that sat on a hill and loomed over all the anorexics of the tri-state area, who trembled when they heard tales of supervised showers and Styrofoam cups filled with chalky liquid nutrition.

"They're going to send you to Seven South," a former patient taunted a friend of mine who was struggling to maintain her weight. It was reminiscent of a child's *you're gonna get it*, or the threat of the boogeyman.

My friend Lisa had been transferred to Cornell (commonly referred to at the Hill as Corn-HELL) again after Silver Hill because her mother wanted her to put on more weight, which a stay at Cornell was guaranteed to accomplish. Laura and I went to visit her, in part just to see the place. We arrived at night. My mother's car crept up the long driveway toward the central building and stopped in front of the main entrance. The halls were dark and eerily quiet, lined with enclaves of earth-toned furniture, walls plastered with pamphlets about addiction, and photo montages of the hospital at various times in its illustrious history. After what seemed like a long walk, we arrived at the door of the unit. Taped to the door were pieces of construction paper decorated with sloppy stars and motivational sayings like "Do your best!" We knocked twice and waited before the door swung furiously open.

"Didn't you see the doorbell?" a scowling African American nurse snapped. We handed the nurse the gifts we had brought Lisa so she could look through them for contraband. The lights were numbingly bright. A radio station blasted popular hits. We found Lisa walking out of the bathroom, laughing with another patient. She sat us down in the living room and told us, with her trademark flippancy, about her doctor's threat to tube her if she didn't eat her dessert, about her comparative anxiety over the two patients who had arrived the day before on stretchers.

On our way out, Lisa pulled a bookshelf away from a wall to show us where the patients dropped the packets of salad dressing they managed to sneak out of the dining room. I watched a young boy with a surly, sunken face shut the door to his room, and for a moment felt pity for his mother, who sat on his bed looking perplexed.

So when, two years later, Jenna sauntered into Adolescent Medicine at Schneider Children's and launched into her tales of Cornell, I put on my headphones and drowned her out with Joni Mitchell. I wanted nothing to do with this legend. My behavior in the months before my admission to

Schneider's had frightened me. I had spent a lot of time uncontrollably visualizing my own funeral and weeping when my parents and brothers stood and said *We will always love you*. I had felt the soft stutter of my aorta and thought ruefully, *Maybe I am going to die, even if I am a normal weight*.

I was trying to hold on to this fear because it was semi-motivating, and it could, I hoped, elevate me above the petty concerns of the disease, the stuff that trips you up—the competition and the comparisons and the hospital social strata and the regret over weight maintained, opportunities for subversive, anorexic behaviors missed. *Maybe if you had made it to* this *weight, things would be different*. If I listened to Jenna's stories, if I believed in the legitimizing power of Corn-HELL, then it would be another strike against me. *If you were* really *sick, they would have sent you there instead of here*. I didn't *want* to be there, or at Schneider's, for that matter, but that wasn't the point; it was a loophole, another way out, and I had in some way started to realize that giving my anorexia *anything* that even *resembled* raw material was dangerous.

Despite my best efforts, I wanted that Cornell merit badge, too, which is why I had to be careful about not listening to Jenna's mock orientation. Now that I actually had some medical complications on my résumé, they didn't seem as noteworthy. Maybe being able to utter the phrase "When I was at Cornell . . ." followed by some terrifying yet pithy anecdote would legitimize me even when cardiac problems would not?

I heard snippets of the stories Jenna told the other girls

who sat around the table, listening intently like children around a campfire reacting to scary yarns with gleeful shrieks. She regaled them with tales about other patients there, about how they did yoga, "but you could only do it if you were at a certain weight," about the constant threat of THE TUBE. She told them about the five-pound rule, which stated that if you lost five pounds after you were discharged, they could toss you right back in.

"I'll bring the patient handbook tomorrow so you guys can see it."

The next day she passed around a fire-engine-red folder filled with papers that listed patient rights in New York state and Seven South treatment protocol. One after the other, the girls asked to see it. Each took the folder quietly and thumbed through the pages, mulling over the details of outdoor privileges and curfews and doctors' visits. The rules, all things considered, weren't that different from the rules at Schneider's, which also had NG tubes and visiting hours and "levels" of privilege you had to eat to reach. I wondered what the other girls were thinking, how they were unpacking, in their minds, the importance of such a place. Was it equivalent to a circle of hell? Did it seem perhaps a better refuge from the world than Schneider's was, a place that offered the safety and predictability of a countryside retreat? Was it a prison where they were likely to be tortured, and was there something about this that was intoxicating to them? Maybe they were like me and believed that if they went to Cornell, or to some other place or reached some other anorexic milestone, they would finally feel the dull thud as they hit their rock bottom. Or was the distinction between these types of places—haven and Guantánamo—blurred enough to render it like the Land of Oz, a place where at any moment, the man behind the curtain might pull it open and reveal to all of us how to click our ruby-red slippers and transport ourselves home?

Jenna was unabashed about her bad behavior outside of Schneider's. As a day patient, she went home at nights and on the weekends, and after her first weekend, she came back to boast that she had consumed only oranges and coffee and screamed at her mother when she tried to follow her to the bathroom.

"I've lost three pounds already," she gloated.

She came to the program late one day, just as we were all entering the Day Hospital building in a line like school-children. As she lurched across the street, she called out to another patient, fever in her voice.

"Alanna! They're sending me back! They're sending me back!"

Whether it was her sense of accomplishment as an eating-disordered person— "I've been hospitalized *so many times!*"—or the thrill of returning to a locus of suffering, she was clearly joyful. And though Schneider's was a hospital and her treatment there would have been an equal notch on her bedpost, as an institution it lacked the prestige of Cornell.

Once you've been hospitalized, it can be difficult to *stop* getting hospitalized for numerous reasons. One is that it can become emblematic of *really* sick, a certain subset of the perverted high of illness, as it did for Jenna. Another reason, though one rarely considered consciously by many, is that the Hospital itself, particularly the Mental Hospital, the Insane Asylum, has always held a chimerical and romantic position in our cultural consciousness. The notion of the nuthouse is scary, yes, all straitjackets and midnight wailing and needles filled with secret serums, but it's also perceived as a place in which patients are ironically more liberated and more honest than they are in the real world. It's a place where struggle is abundant, and always meaningful.

"Our hospital was famous and had housed many great poets and singers," Susanna Kaysen writes of McLean Hospital, the institution favored by Boston Brahmins that has treated, at one point or another, James Taylor, Robert Lowell, Fredrick Law Olmstead (who also designed the grounds), and, of course, Sylvia Plath. Anne Sexton, famously competitive with Sylvia Plath both as a poet and a depressive, chose McLean as the site of her poetry workshop because it held "an odd glamour for her," wrote biographer Diane Wood Middlebrook. She later became a patient there less than a year before she committed suicide.

"Did the hospital specialize in poets and singers, or was it that poets and singers specialized in madness?" Kaysen asks. She never does answer her own question. Janet Frame, perhaps New Zealand's most famous poet and wordsmith, describes her struggle with "schizophrenia" (quotes are included as she almost certainly never met the diagnostic criteria) and the way in which she came to treasure her diagnosis quite brilliantly in the second installment of her autobiographical trilogy, *An Angel at My Table*. A pudgy, frizzy-haired, shy aspiring poet, Frame found herself physically and emotionally adrift when she arrived to study at university in the mid-1940s. She attempted suicide—she survived the mild overdose without medical intervention—and then wrote about it in a class paper. Her teacher promptly had her admitted to the local psychiatric hospital, where she was eventually diagnosed as schizophrenic. She had never heard of schizophrenia before, so her diagnosis confused her, but she began to apply it to herself and use it to her advantage. Frame explains to her reader how it seemed to be her only expression of otherness and special-ness, the most direct line between herself and cultural lumi-naries, such as van Gogh. It was an opportunity to feel rebellious; before the suicide attempt and hospitalization, she was frequently described as lovely and mild mannered, and anyone who has ever felt like a nonentity in this way knows how frustrating such labels can be.

"My place was set, then, at the terrible feast," she writes. "I had no illusions about 'greatness' but at least I could endow my work and—when necessary—my life with the mark of my schizophrenia . . . a disease interesting enough to be my ally in my artistic efforts and to ensure, provided I maintained the correct symptoms, that I had the continued audience."

Her illness also allowed her to express herself when stressed and to wave a distinctly white flag and call her life to a halt when she wished to retreat back to an institution, which she saw as both a prison and a safe haven. In these institutions, she felt comfortable and accepted among the eccentric but inclusive community of the ill. On the outside, she worried that if she were to entirely discard the cachet of the label, she would lose the constant support and vigilance of others. "I continued to fear that I might once again be left with no one to talk to, that is, in a 'normal' state of nearness to mental breakdown, for I was on the usual adolescent path of worry and wondering how to 'cope' with everyday living; yet, strangely, in order to lessen my anxiety, I found myself forced to choose a more distinctly signposted path, where my journey drew attention and so, I found, drew more practical help."

Frame was in and out of psychiatric hospitals for eight years and high up on the waiting list for a leucotomy operation (prefrontal lobotomy) when the superintendent of the hospital announced to her that she had won a writing prize and as a result, he decided not to operate. After a substantial time on less strict wards and in the hospital's occupational-therapy program, Frame was allowed to go home. She was never readmitted to an institution and became New Zealand's foremost female writer.

• • •

I WAS EVENTUALLY HOSPITALIZED AT CORNELL NOT ONCE but twice. The first time was not long after my stay at Schneider's—I returned to school a week late after spending the whole Christmas vacation at the hospital, but I knew pretty early on that it wasn't going to go very well. When my parents dropped me off at my dorm, I turned back toward my father and let out tears I had been holding during the drive to school. "It'll be okay," he said, and then left.

I lost weight quickly and without much effort during those few months back at school, mostly because my metabolism had been bolstered by the regular feeding at Schneider's. By March, I was back below goal weight, and though my cognition was far better than it had been in December, my therapist wanted me admitted again to raise my weight, this time at Cornell. The first admission was uneventful, but during my second admission, around Halloween of 2004, I met a girl who was, for a time, the most famous anorexic in Manhattan, the legendary Lily Brown. Our stays there overlapped only by a few days, but it was enough to establish an anorexic idolatry in me that would last for years. We spoke briefly the night of my admission despite the fact that I had explicitly told myself not to make friends with anyone on the unit. It would only trip me up, I thought, and I needed to have blinders on, so desperate was I to regain my strength, for the first and perhaps only time in my disease's eight years.

The pale, relatively healthy-looking girl with a long braid of brown hair running down her back asked me questions about myself: my name, my age, if I had ever been in the hospital before, and if so where. Unlike Kristin, who years earlier had pressed me for my waist size then grabbed her own pelvic bones, there seemed nothing prurient about Lily, so I answered her. Kelsey, twenty, yes, at Silver Hill in 2000, Long Island Jewish (Schneider's) in 2003, Cornell in 2003, and then, obviously, Cornell once again, in 2004.

"How long have you been here?" I asked.

"Two and a half months," she said.

Immediately I knew that she was a serious anorexic, because Cornell was a strict facility. If you were inpatient for more than a month, most likely you came in at a very low weight. I envisioned Lily's large blue eyes bulging a bit further out of their sockets.

"Wow. That's a long time."

"Last time I was here for three and a half months," she said.

Nothing about her tone seemed haughty, which is rare for an anorexic talking about her hospitalizations.

Well, they wanted to send me to a residential facility, but I was a medical risk. Read: I am awesome at starving myself.

My parents forced me to come here. Read: I don't care about anyone else's concerns because I'm *hard-core.*

The doctor says that if I lose five pounds after I'm discharged she'll send me right back. Read: get an eyeful of me now, as the powers that be will never let me get so sick again.

But Lily was calm about it all, cordial, in fact. We talked about doctors we both knew and then about New York, which is where she also lived. The only time I ever saw her facade of stability crack was when I asked her where she went to school.

"An all-girl's private school on the East Side," she said.

"Which one?"

She reluctantly answered me, and only then did it

occur to me that it was probably embarrassing for her to tell me. She probably hadn't actually been to school in ages, maybe didn't have many friends.

Lily kept to herself. She ate (supervised) outside of the dining room for reasons that were never clear, and she never attended group therapy or spoke openly about her eating disorder. Everything I learned about her was passed on by other patients.

"Lily was so bad she had a feeding tube at home. She went to school like that, with just the little end sticking out of her nose!"

"Lily never finishes her Ensure."

"I asked her why she never went to group, and she just said she didn't want to and that nobody made her anymore."

Her parents were wealthy and had agreed to finance a six-month stay at a very respectable hospital in California. The morning she was to leave, she didn't drink any of her Ensure and smiled like a dope when she gave the Styrofoam cup back to the nurse. I went out on a limb and asked her about not finishing her supplement.

"Guess there's no pressure to drink it today, huh?"

"My parents will probably take me to Starbucks or something. I just want to have a normal breakfast." She smiled as she said the last part.

I searched her face for any indication that she was lying, any conspiratorial glimmer in her eyes, but there was nothing. Most every eating-disordered person I knew left at least a small window open for external validation. Can a denial be so thorough as to be rendered impenetrable? Even the staff had given up and no longer seemed chagrined about lack of caring. I thought of the line by John Berryman, the stereotypically tortured poet who committed suicide: "I am so wise I had my mouth sewn shut." And it was this that I envied at first, not her body, as she looked almost normal by this point. Her résumé intrigued me, sure (four hospitals, feeding tubes, a quick transfer to a six-month program), but even further, the strength of her feigned ignorance, her refusal to be made complicit or ambivalent, the relieving detachment and unity of spirit I believed she must feel as a result of this. Lily was anorexic and no one was going to break into that fortress. Me, I begged for armies to attack by night.

A month or so after I was discharged, I heard through the grapevine that Lily had left California early and was back at her parents' apartment on Fifth Avenue. This gossip came from other anorexics with whom I was in group therapy and from health care professionals, practically all of whom had treated Lily at one point or another. A friend of mine had seen her when she had the feeding tube outside of the hospital, a concept absolutely mind-boggling to me. Another's doctor said that other anorexics who went to school with Lily talked about how sick she looked in their sessions. Someone else had seen her jogging in place on a Madison Avenue corner. Her mother had an eating disorder, too, another said.

"To her, it's like a secret, and if she talks about it, it's like she's betraying her eating disorder," I was told.

Something about secrets got me by the throat. Secrets

are mysterious, and mystery is a form of beauty, and everyone wants to be beautiful. I could never keep my own secrets;
I just gave away all the beauty I had, which wasn't much to
begin with, to anyone who asked.

The next time I saw Lily, she was exiting an office in
the complex where my nutritionist's practice was located.
Before she came out, I somehow knew she was there. I knew
it was time for her entrance. She looked surprised to see me
and thin—very, very thin. We both gave a start. She held the
rim of a bottle of orange juice with the tips of her fingers as
if repulsed by coming even that close to anything of caloric
value.

"Do you remember me?" I asked.

"Yeah, hi! How are you?" The same cheer despite her
wan appearance, which was nauseating even to me, who
craved bone visibility. Two other girls were sitting in the
waiting room, and I could feel them waiting to exhale. Even
the arms of the chairs seemed to stiffen in response to Lily's
silhouette. Later that evening, I cried heavy tears because of
how she had looked, because it was terrifying, because I
wanted to be her and yet I was repulsed by her. It seemed
that the only way I would have any peace from that struggle,
after all that time, would be if I got thin enough. At least
then I'd be able to rule one out.

Over the course of the next few months, I saw her in
that office complex numerous times. I wanted her to just
once talk to me about her eating disorder, just once tell me
she was having a hard time or that she hated her therapist
for making her gain weight or something, anything. Instead,

we talked about her work at a college science lab. She told me she was reading *Anna Karenina*. She bought new Uggs. I noticed scabs on her pale hands that never seemed to heal.

During one session with a therapist, I have it on good account, she stopped in the middle of an innocuous conversation and said, "I don't want to go back into the hospital."

The therapist, surprised she was broaching the topic, responded, "And why is that?" expecting Lily to answer that she didn't want to gain weight or that she hated eating.

"Because when I go, I'm never the skinny one."

• • •

BY MY SECOND ADMISSION TO CORNELL WESTCHESTER, I FELT the allure of the insane asylum, the aura it emanated, lessen, and I started to wonder how different, really, it was on either side of the locked door. Did it mean anything about anyone's fundamental being that they had graced the threshold of the psych ward? Were my ward-mates more likely to win a Pulitzer or answer a religious calling or have an impressive artistic portfolio than those who had never been diagnosed with a mental illness? During that second admission, I met an aide named Michaela, whom some might describe as a "hipster." She had boy-short hair and wore glasses that made her look studious and combat boots and rode her bike everywhere. One day, during a "courtyard"—cigarette break—another patient asked her about her tattoos. She pointed out each one and explained what they meant ("The plus sign is to remind me to always be positive . . ."), and then mentioned nonchalantly that she had done them herself. I thought about pricking the skin with a needle and rubbing ink over the wound and feeling . . . what, afterward? Calm? Exhilarated? The way one feels after getting a tattoo, after self-mutilating? Bingeing and purging a month's worth of food? After weeks of fasting? Why was this okay for Michaela to do and not us? Because she lived in Brooklyn? Because she cut symbols, shapes with purpose and meaning that could be interpreted by observers? Not unlike some of the rest of us, like Catie in *Thin,* who carved the Japanese symbol for pain onto her hip. Is it because her symbol meant pain and Michaela's meant something happy, something optimistic, that Catie's rendered her a nutcase and Michaela's made her "hip"?

Or Rebecca, another patient at Cornell, who burned herself with cigarettes that left hauntingly round scars all over her arms and legs. She told people who asked that she had been in a car accident, though anyone with half a brain would have guessed otherwise, as the wounds resembled those of a strange medieval disease, a pox or leprosy that had stigmatized her, in some way, as untouchable, separate, or maybe even special.

Rebecca told me once that she became anxious when the scars started to disappear, when they seemed to be "leaving her," as her father had when he passed away from a brain tumor when she was ten years old. These circles meant something to her, too, as much, maybe, as Catie's symbol for pain or Michaela's plus sign.

Is it because tattooing is an industry? Is that why it's okay? Anorexia and self-mutilation have become commoditized as well. Look at *Thin.* Simple exhibition of these diseases is done for monetary profit. Manifestations of this commercialization of aberrant behavior run the gamut from the basely pornographic to the highbrow. Vanessa Beecroft is an artist known for arranging models scantily clad in haute couture lingerie in geometric patterns and having them stand until they collapse onto cold marble floors in front of hushed spectators. Beecroft's springboard for her artistic career? Her eating disorder, ED-NOS, which caused her to keep methodical food diaries of her macrobiotic intake and then bring the diaries into art school as source material. And she ended up in the Whitney as opposed to Payne Whitney. Where is she, on the spectrum of pathological, of certifiable? Where is Chris Burden, the performance artist who nailed himself to his Volkswagen and had his assistant shoot him in the arm? Where is Isocrates, the Greek rhetorician who starved himself to death after a Greek military defeat, or Gandhi, who often fasted in order to calm civil strife, or, in other words, get what he wanted? Where is Marina Abramovic? Where are Michaela and Jenna and Lily?

Where am I?

Another situation in which I wonder where to draw the line:

I remembered the first time I saw Layla.

My dad dropped me off next to the two stone eagles that stood regally by the steps that led up to the door to Silver Hill. A fat, greasy woman sat between to them. Huge circles of black eyeliner surrounded her eyes, making them look concave, evil. Smoke sifted through her yellowed teeth and shielded her fleshy face from my stare.

Sandra, a bulimic who had been at the hospital for a

long time and was a trove of hospital stories, folklore, and gossip, told me later that the woman's name was Layla and that she had been in this x-dollar-a-day (read: really, really expensive) hospital for thirty years. Rumor had it that she was a former model who had taken a hit of bad acid during a Rolling Stones concert, and Mick Jagger had been paying for her hospitalization ever since.

"They may have had an affair," Sandra said.

It was better than television.

Sandra told me tidbits about Layla. She wore the black eyeliner, ironically, to ward *off* evil spirits and allegedly wouldn't take a shower because she thought she was a glass of orange juice and was afraid she'd dilute. We thought this was hilarious.

Layla's mother, Olivia, had also been in the hospital for over a decade, though not even the all-knowing Sandra could tell me why. She was ancient, confined to a wheelchair, and had her own nurse. She always sat in the dining room extension, at a little table behind our table. She would moan, "I'm dying, I'm dying," while her nurse would chat loudly about her current diet with any staff member who'd listen.

"I've really lost weight on that Hollywood juice thing," she marveled nasally while we cringed at the next table, slurping our mandatory soup.

I heard Layla talk only once, during a fire drill. The tech on duty had led us out the fire escape and down the stairs to the Doctors' Office Building, a cottage that snuggled up next to what was known as "Main House." Lisa,

Laura, and I shuffled our feet on the snowy ground and wondered aloud how long it would be until we were permitted to go back upstairs.

"These things usually don't last very long. Maybe half an hour."

We tried to keep our jaws from dropping open. The words had come out of the mouth of Layla, the silent lady of the manor. Yet her voice was clear and sane, and her statement certain.

Cut to: the year after I graduated from college I became fascinated with the Hotel Chelsea, a storied New York City hotel where, oddly enough, my hair salon was located. The hotel was in the middle of a hostile takeover of sorts, so it was constantly in the press, and I read everything published about it. The articles named the various artists who had lived there over the centuries, the great books that had been written within the thick cement walls, the sexual dalliances of its notorious patrons, the drugs taken and angst-ridden love ballads sung and murders committed. It was very often compared to a madhouse. In one of my readings I came across a notice of a biography that had recently been completed about an oddball female artist who had been a longtime resident and whose painting still hung near the stairwell landing on the third floor.

"Vali's appearance was always striking and idiosyncratic: with her bushy red hair, long gypsy robes, heavy jewelry and facial tattoos—along with her black eye makeup, designed to ward off evil spirits—one would think she probably warded off a good many mortal souls as well."

I couldn't believe it. She was exactly like Layla, only touted as a monumental eccentric, a crazy genius, an artist whose best canvas was her body. Would that woman of my memory have been a marginally famous urban personality had the context of her illness (parents, education, environment, whatever) been different? Is one man's beautiful madcap icon another's repulsive, goose-fleshed mental patient? Again: does it mean anything about any individual's fundamental being that they have graced the threshold of the psych ward? This was the point at which I came firmly down on the side of: not really. Some people know how to market themselves better, perhaps, or can visit the nation of insanity without ever filing for citizenship.

But it can feel after the fact like there was something cogent and powerful about the experience, about the Place itself, that it *meant something*, and that *you* meant something more as a mad person than you ever will as a sane one. And this nostalgia doesn't ever quite fade.

When I first began writing this book, I told two friends from group therapy my plan to return to all the places where I was hospitalized in order to facilitate the writing process. Both of them had also been inpatient at Schneider's and expressed enthusiastic interest in joining me. I was surprised at this, especially considering their voiced hatred of the hospital: its gargantuan buildings, strangling hallways, dirty little windowless rooms. Then again, I, too, was voluntarily going back and was pretty sure it would do nothing I told myself it would, like jump-start my memory or bring emotions I might have buried to the surface. Deep down, I knew

I wanted to go back just to see it again, to be close to the center of the flame for one brief moment, like in later high school years, when, bored, I would drive past Silver Hill and wonder who was in there now and what they were feeling. Why did we all want to return so badly? Because returning to the hospital, we thought, would remind us of the moments of real danger we experienced, and would bring us back to the hub of the horror and rejuvenate us so we could once again face the world, our lives. Somehow we continued to believe that it is in the moments we are close to death that we feel most alive, and in the depths of our misery that we are most complete. Thus when it was over and we were warm in our own beds, eating our breakfasts and walking freely down the city streets, we often asked ourselves with a sighing disappointment: *Is this really it?*

"I want to go on a raid," a war-sick American soldier confessed to a writer friend of mine. "I want something to blow up. I want something to change today."

Or, as Dorothy Parker put it, "They sicken of the calm, who knew the storm."

That's what we think, anyway. The hospital environment never provides the satisfaction one may hope for. It only does that in retrospect. A college acquaintance named Amelia bounced from one end of the manic spectrum to the other, binging and purging and starving and grasping at the hands of friends (anyone, really) for help or reassurance. She wanted to hit a bottom, and thought maybe a hospitalization would do that. She found her six days at Cornell, however, lacking. "It's just a bunch of girls sitting around knitting and whining about food," she lamented to me. But what had she expected? *ER*'s County General, with its handsome, caring doctors, plotlines rife with opportunity for Aristotelian catharsis-by-proxy, bolstered by a well-composed soundtrack?

The grass is always greener on the other side of the stone wall topped with barbed wire.

When Kristin, the tween who had desperately emulated me at Silver Hill, was discharged into the day program, the three inpatients left, Lisa, Laura, and I, anorexics all, were thrilled. We wouldn't have to deal with her antics during meals, the way she casually threw chicken across the room or crawled on the floor sobbing when she felt sick. She was annoying and troublesome, and we were not sad to see her go.

Kristin went home on a Thursday. We all patted her on the back and wished her well before dashing around the near-empty unit like children with the house to ourselves. We spent a remarkably calm two days drawing on placemats with crayons, wishing aloud for peanut butter and jelly, watching reruns on television. Then midday Saturday, the fire drill blasted and our heads shot up from our coloring. We were ushered outside. This was when we heard Layla's voice. It was an exciting day, all things considered.

"I hope they figure this out soon," Paul, the psych tech, said. "We have a new admit coming up to Main Three."

A new admit? We looked at each other nervously. I can't speak for my comrades, but I was thinking optimistically. Maybe it would be someone catatonically depressed and mercifully unobtrusive.

When we returned to the unit we waited nervously for the new patient. After a few minutes we heard the door to Main 3 click and saw a little girl with mouse-brown straw hair. She was wearing blue jeans and a familiar purple *The Fantastiks!* sweatshirt. It was Kristin. She had lasted a mere two days at home and quickly announced that she was not here for an eating disorder anymore.

"I'm here for self-mutilation now," she said.

She explained that her father had refused to play in the snow with her so she had gone to the second story of her house and jumped out a window, twisting her ankle and frightening her parents. A few bandages peeked out from beneath the sleeves of her sweatshirt. She ate her food quietly and at a reasonable pace, yet still with that caged-animal look in her eyes.

On Sunday she asked Paul for the box of art supplies and the scissors. She asked for those specifically. He gave them to her without question. I watched her walk out of the dayroom toward her bedroom, carrying the plastic Tupperware filled with markers. I knew she was going to cut, but I didn't stop her or tell Paul my suspicions. I was irritated by the return of her transparent antics, convinced there wasn't anything deep behind this imminent outburst, that it was just some way to create a din, to get a reaction in hopes that the staff would force new rules upon her, have conferences about her, just think about *her*. She was like a rebellious baby back in her favorite playpen, anxious to see how much commotion she could cause. Whether the attention garnered from the act was negative or positive didn't matter to her, as it often doesn't to babies testing their efficacy; what matters is that there is a reaction *period*.

Sure enough, a few moments after she had exited, she wandered back to the nurses' station.

"Paul, I cut," she said, before bursting into loud tears.

He bandaged her up and put her on Sharps and Dayroom Observation and informed the rest of the staff on Monday morning what had happened. As we shuffled through groups, we watched the patients look from Kristin's face to one another's back to hers in sheer astonishment when she announced she no longer had an eating disorder. Now she was a cutter.

Lisa and I sequestered ourselves by the phone one afternoon and called Iris, a patient who had been kicked out of the program a few weeks earlier for giving Kristin a rock she could put in her underwear to help tip the scale.

"She should look at my arms," Iris scoffed.

She probably already has, I thought, *and that may be part of the problem.*

When Kristin walked back through the door that fateful Saturday, I wondered to myself, *Why? Why would she do something so stupid and childish, something she knew would land her back in a place she claimed to hate so much?* Despite all her transgressions, I still considered Kristin a "real" anorexic, and real anorexics wouldn't do such things. Real anorexics avoid hospitals and doctors and Dayroom Obs at all costs. They desire invisibility. But I hadn't yet experienced the real world Post-Hospitalization, and I didn't know, then, the frightening, Bergman-esque silence that res-onates around you when you find yourself truly alone, war-denless, the very real and utter impotence you feel when you skip a snack and smirk and look around and realize that no one, absolutely no one, is watching. Years later on long, lonely walks down wet city streets, I would realize that the terror of the real world was not that your sadness *seemed* to matter so much less there, but that it actually did.

CHAPTER 10

DISTANCES FROM DEATH

My friend Tomas used to tell me often that he wanted to join the army even though the war was something he protested vehemently. This was disconcerting to hear, not only because his well-being was important to me, but because his logic seemed flawed. He believed that his life had always been too comfortable and that he was detached from his emotions. Even worse, he believed he was unable to grasp his own mortality. In antiquated masculine terminology, he believed he had become *soft*. He, too, wondered what Walker Percy, the southern writer and existential philosopher, did in his book *The Delta Factor:* "Why is the good life which men have achieved in the twentieth century so bad that only news of world catastrophes, assassinations, plane crashes, mass murders, can divert one from the sadness of ordinary mornings?"

Tomas thought that maybe, if confronted with the brutal and inescapable reality of bombs-blowing-limbs-off and here-today-gone-tomorrow, he would be *forced* into complete awareness, unable to take things for granted anymore—in a word, *enlightened*. He would return home and approach his life with all the zest and vigor of a man who had been given a second chance. He would acquire the knowledge of the resurrected.

I wasn't confused by his logic, nor did I think it strange. It seemed to me a pretty common desire, this wish for forced and lasting epiphany. Human beings actively put themselves into dangerous, potentially life-threatening situations all the time in order to "feel alive." They climb high mountains with minimal oxygen or jump from airplanes or shoot up heroin or hurt themselves to see if they still feel. *New York Times* columnist David Carr, who wrote about his addiction to crack cocaine in his memoir *The Night of the Gun,* says, "The objective is to walk right up to the edge of an overdose, to get as high as humanly possible without actually dying." It's a trope in life and in literature; Ray Bradbury's story "The Lost City of Mars" is summarized by *New York Times* writer Tim Kreider as a tale "in which a man finds a miraculous machine that enables him to experience his own violent death over and over again, as many times as he likes—in locomotive collisions, race car crashes, exploding rockets—until he emerges flayed of all his free-floating guilt and unconscious longing for death, forgiven and free, finally alive." The belief that proximity to death will bring one closer to life carries within it the assumption

that existence post–turning-from-the-white-light will be somehow easier, that issues of morality will be less ambiguous,
that the "right" decision will be clearer and the positive
viewpoint the instinctual one, always.

I can relate. As a child, I prayed that something would
jerk me from what I believed was textbook suburban seda-
tion, my world of comfort. My liturgies presented themselves as slide shows: me in a bloody car accident or the
victim of a kidnapping or suffering from some horrendously
painful illness or something, anything that would help me
(and those in my immediate universe) to understand, once
and for all, that I was a real live person in a fragile, human
body and that all *this* was not a joke or a figment of my
imagination, but immensely consequential. None of these
terrible fates befell me, however, and so I felt compelled to
actively seek out *the edge* with the help of a companion that,
to an adolescent girl, seemed to also hold so much social,
romantic, and emotional prestige. What I hadn't realized at
the time was that this companion was downright evil, and
would pretend to quench my thirst for knowledge with a
few meager drops, faux facts, empty epiphanies. Every time
I came to the edge, it would tiptoe beside me and whisper
snidely in my ear: *Are you sure this is really the edge? Perhaps go a bit further . . . just to be sure.*

Other anorexics I knew felt this, too, wished through
their disease to look into the abyss, if only for a moment. I
recall a day after I was discharged from Silver Hill. I was attending school but left a bit early every day to go to the hospital for the afternoon program, including group therapy,

snacks, and dinner. My mother had a car service pick me up at school because neither she nor my father could leave work for long enough to pick me up and drive me to the program. I would nap in the back of those black town cars. Every so often a driver would ask me why I was going to Silver Hill.

"Do you volunteer there or something?" the driver asked me one day.

I said yes, and remember thinking it was strange that I had lied. Wasn't I proud of my anorexia?

That afternoon, Laura and Lisa and I were discussing what would need to happen for us to be "satisfied" as anorexics.

"I want to be, like, revived from a heart attack," Lisa said.

The other thing I didn't know, and neither, it seems, did Tomas or my fellow patients, was that this is not the way epiphanies by trauma happen. The brain is a remarkable organism hell-bent on protecting itself; in a moment of fear or despair it deems too intense, it will soften the blow in order to allow the body to continue to put one foot in front of the other. As a result, the traumatic moment may be dulled, the action happening at a distance, as if on a screen in a movie. When you get back to the barracks at night, you laugh about it, or you drink a beer to forget, or you move about as if through molasses, trying but failing to truly understand, internalize, *feel* what has really occurred.

"School's under lockdown because of a terrorist attack," Orah wrote to me in an e-mail while studying in

Jerusalem. "I was actually in the area of the attack around 5ish today . . . Crazy how things play out. A bunch of girls were scared and in tears but these things don't really bring tears to me. Maybe they should? I def feel it but . . . I don't know." She, like my wannabe soldier friend, seemed to be operating under the assumption that there are things that ought to instantly shake the ground she walked on, that anything meaningful would do so, and if it didn't, the flaw was either something in the event itself or, more likely, in her.

Even if you don't "dissociate" in some manner, if you remain in real time throughout the harrowing moments, it still takes a while for the ramifications of such traumatic or near-death experiences to really penetrate. Only when the brain realizes it is safe can it release its pent-up energy and begin to wrestle with the messy soup of reactions to witnessing or experiencing something genuinely terrifying. This moment, sadly, can coincide with the one in which the war anecdotes and snapshots and tales of blood splatter have lost their novelty, their glamour. This is the moment at which the victim of trauma relaxes, tries to shake off his attachment to reminiscence and begins to crave nothing short of stability. The night is quiet. There is no gunfire, no screaming, no hands that reach out to grab you. You are safe at last. And yet . . .

"Now dreams occurring in traumatic neuroses have the characteristic of repeatedly bringing the patient back into the situation of his accident, a situation from which he wakes up in another fright," Freud wrote.

In sleep, my anorexia was everywhere. I guided peers

through endless freezer aisles, instructing them how to calculate the servings of dairy in one cup of ice cream. Ashy skeletons with NG tubes dragged poles over the cobblestone paths
of my university. The bags atop the poles shook from the
bumpy ground as the skeletons walked determinedly toward
no destination. Nurses forced us into tiny bathrooms, shoved
enemas at us, and watched us insert them to make sure we followed through. We cried in pain and humiliation, and afterward we ran into our bedrooms and stuffed the cracks under
the doors with dark rags, knowing somehow that the fumes
of anorexia would seep in if we didn't *hurry, hurry, hurry*.
Sometimes I dreamed I returned to the hospital by choice,
wanting to give someone a tour so they would have firsthand
knowledge, wanting to see for myself what had changed there.
I would bump into Lily Brown in the hallway, lock arms with
her, and whisper, "I've missed you so much." We would walk
to the spot where we could look out the window at the courtyard and see babies writhing in the grass or everyone with
whom I've ever been hospitalized, and I would put a hand to
the glass and weep because I couldn't touch them.

But mostly, I dreamed of escape. I bolted across a field
during a cigarette break, leaves crunching beneath my feet,
or sneaked out an open door, or pried open a loose vent and
crawled through. Afterward I would have to chop off my
hair, or find a hiding place or dig a computer-monitoring
chip out from beneath my skin. They could be anywhere,
people looking to bring me back there, and so if I found myself on the roof of a building and I saw their binoculars
sticking out from the foliage around me, I would have no

choice but to jump. And I would wake up sweating, back in Freud's "situation of the accident."

But it was no accident, this baffling thing with which I contended over and over again. It was my fault. I wanted it, the thrill of teetering on the edge, the *experience*. After all, I had enlisted in the army. I had wanted to fight. I just hadn't realized that the enemy would keep fighting long after I had surrendered.

• • •

TO GET SO CLOSE TO DEATH THAT YOU FEEL REBORN: THIS IS the goal. But the paradoxical thing is that by tapping the tip of your demise, by courting it, you often find yourself with what appears to be the means to achieve immortality, something that everyone figuratively wants. We want to be remembered after we are gone, and a story, particularly a printed and bound one, is a great way to assure that will happen. And the more spectacular the story, the more marketable it is. And the more marketable, the more likely it is to be packaged, thus making it more difficult to destroy, less likely to become a whispered one-liner drowned out by the surf.

> Read me, do not let me die!
> Search the fading letters, finding
> Steadfast in the broken binding
> All that once was I!

Edna St. Vincent Millay writes in "The Poet and His Book." This is my legacy, my bid for immortality. This is what I, in natural human desperation, want to leave behind.

In the June 29, 2009, issue of *Us Weekly* magazine, the main headline reads "*The Hills* Made Me Bulimic." The bullets beneath it outline what the article will examine in further detail: "The agony of working with 'skinny girls,'" "5,000-calorie-a-day bingeing," "How she tried to kill herself." The text is superimposed on the image of a bikini-clad, dolled-up Stephanie Pratt, the focus of the article, the girl whose spot on a reality TV show "made" her bulimic.

The content of the article is irrelevant. Its existence is the thing. Broken down: the goal is to be seen and thus be affirmed. Beneath this self-indulgent exposure is a desire to believe in one's ability to affect another. See me. Hear me. Buy me. Prove me to *myself.* To be seen is a common desire of the eating-disordered, the irony of which has been analyzed elsewhere to the point of exhaustion. Desperation lives in the request to be looked at, in the baring of a sick body, in the public confession made by megaphone. Deep down there is a plea to be recognized and kept alive, if only in the digital archives. Stephanie Pratt was the least famous cast member of *The Hills,* and by doing this cover story, she pushed herself into the foreground, if only for a moment. By responding to her cheap confession, our culture is confirming fears endemic to Stephanie Pratt and so many other eating-disordered people, the ones that reverberate off the walls of treatment centers far and wide: that "normal" or "good" is the worst thing you can be. Meaningless. Stable. Boring. The nonromantic kind of gossamer. Nothing.

I look normal now!

My eating disorder is the only thing special about me"

No one will like me if I'm fat.

If I'm not sick, everyone will forget about me.

Maybe this is true in Hollywood, but probably not even there. In the real world, people forget about anorexics all the time. You see them, the forgotten ones, in the dingiest of psychiatric wards, barren, wobbly middle-aged women with the drawn faces and gray teeth of the elderly. Vacant-eyed from shock treatments, these women ask the same questions over and over again, brains atrophied by years of malnutrition. "Where is my baby? Where is my baby?" They thumb pictures of infants left behind, grown children who have long since moved on.

"Further, if the starvation persists over many years, the psychic effects are integrated into the personality, and the overall picture may become indistinguishable from the borderline syndrome, or even schizophrenia," writes Hilde Bruch in *The Golden Cage*. And it's true. These wild-eyed ones don't write books; they don't give testimonies on talk shows. They're shut up in state institutions, left to try gouging holes in their arms with fingernails filed to stubs, shrieking and slamming their fists into walls. They're giggled at by the younger set, those still pretty and viable, those who push from their minds the realization that regardless of genes or upbringing or cultural triggers or education or *anything*, if they stay with their dearly beloved Ana, one day they will be them, the ones who are *really* crazy, the ones who are beyond hope.

Nobody visits, nobody calls—maybe family members, but often not even them. These sad, prematurely old women perch throughout the wards like dusty ornaments. They have been left behind, and those who did the leaving cannot be blamed.

A woman named Sigrid was on the unit at Cornell the first time I was a patient there. She was twenty-nine, but even in hindsight, it's impossible to conceive of her as this age. Judging by appearance alone, she could have been sixty. Sigrid had been hospitalized at Cornell because she had run away from so many other facilities that her family and treatment team wanted her on a locked unit. Because she was on bed rest, she spent most of her time in her room, playing Scattergories with another patient and me before we got tired of her whining. Sigrid led a little campaign against what she considered to be cruel treatment of the patients: the fact that we were only allowed one flavor of liquid nutritional supplement. During group we tried to tell her we thought she was stalling the feeding process. In response, she said how hard it was to drink the supplement when she had to watch Leta, another patient, eat less and less every day. Furious with the staff and with us, Sigrid sulked all afternoon, and when we protested that they were just trying to help us, she shot back, "If we want to die, they should just let us die." One quick look at each person's face told me that most of us, in fact, didn't actually want to die.

Eventually Sigrid's father, a wealthy businessman from the Dominican Republic, had her transferred to yet another hospital, a facility in the pastoral backwoods of Connecticut. It was a more open facility, but even so, I believed she was most likely forever condemned to that pathetic diaspora of the aging patients who weep over scrambled eggs and tighter jeans, a ghost in my peripheral vision.

I glanced over Sigrid's shoulder at Cornell once when she was typing on an ancient computer someone had donated to the unit. She was writing her memoir, *My Life with Anorexia*. Chapter 1 was entitled "Why Me?" Her life and her story most likely languish on this computer, now in storage in the basement of that giant hospital, one more forgotten narrative among many.

CHAPTER 11

ATTEMPTING NARRATIVE

ON BEAUTY, REGULARITY AND FORM

My need (and others', too) to fit my disease into a coherent narrative, something teleological and palatable, something with a *conclusion,* made me want to examine my life and pick out the places where I as the omniscient narrator had employed literary devices.

ALLUSION

You'll see mine, sprinkled throughout, just as you'll find them in Hornbacher's work.

From *Wasted:* "You can, perhaps, foresee a series of terrifically dramatic relationships in my future, all ending with me in an Ophelian heap on my quilt."

FORESHADOWING

After we both had been discharged from Silver Hill, when I was seventeen, Laura called me one day to tell me about a dream she had.

"You were in my dream last night."

"What happened?" I asked.

"We were at the Hill, and Aubrey was taking us for a walk. It was you and Lisa and me. Everything looked pretty much the same except there was a huge hill at the end of the circle. When we got to the end of the walk, you tripped and fell all the way down the hill, and then I woke up."

ALLEGORY

One morning during my first stay at Cornell, I walked into the dayroom before breakfast. My hair was still wet. Two patients, a teenage girl and an ancient-looking thirty-year-old, were already there. The television station playing was CNN. It showed footage from Iraq, of civilians marching into a town square and toppling a huge statue of Saddam Hussein. The Iraqis were cheering and waving flags and smiling into the camera. I wrote an essay about this after I returned to school. The last line was some stretch of a sentimental point, something relating the collapse of the Iraqi dictatorship to the collapse of my own internal tyrant.

But the allegory hadn't collapsed, it seemed, and less than two years later, I was back in the hospital. Was this dramatic irony on the part of the omniscient narrator? Once again my world was relegated to those three tall, thin hallways-cum-rooms, that gray dining area with its one tiny, grime-covered window. Our nation's troops had been in Iraq for the entire two-year interlude between hospital stays and had failed to find weapons of mass destruction. From that same spot on the couch, I watched as Bush was reelected, and said aloud, "We are all doomed."

And now this moment that felt somehow climactic and conclusive has been lost in a sea of political scandals and harrowing international conflicts and small individual tragedies.

ARCHETYPE

I don't know if Jung covered this, but it's "Sad, Lost Little Girl." It is most definitely a cultural trope. A favorite artistic manifestation of this idea is *Alice in Wonderland*. Marya Hornbacher claims her, lifts entire passages from *this* little girl's tale. Sarah Haight, a contributor to *Going Hungry*, tells the story of how the patients on the psych ward at the hospital where she interned called her Alice because of her long blond hair. Susanna Kaysen questions the entire concept of going mad by repeatedly referring to Carroll's make-believe world. "But I wasn't simply going nuts," she says, "tumbling down a shaft into Wonderland."

Why do we have such an affinity for Alice? Her precociousness, innocence, wherewithal in the face of a foreign, baffling, and sometimes dangerous world? Her long blond hair? Her pretty blue dress?

Will anyone ever tire of her?

I want to be Alice, too. I am blond and small in stature. My face is full and youthful. I've always liked adventures. Maybe we're cosmically connected? Should I play that part? I have a friend, also small, also blond, also a former anorexic, who twitches with envy whenever I get the comparison. I get it often, and I gloat inside, a little. For the record, I find I have far more adventures now, being healthy, than I ever did sick.

An extreme example of this self-characterizing we do:

In college I knew a girl who, after one summer break, came back *as* Edie Sedgwick, the painfully beautiful Warhol superstar who died at twenty-eight after a lifetime of struggling with eating disorders and drug abuse. Edie is a common icon for the young, the aspiring waif, the enamored-of-tragedy. I had gone through my Edie phase a few years before, bought three pairs of chandelier earrings and read her patchwork biography by Jean Stein. I was only half stunned to discover that we had been hospitalized at two of the same psychiatric hospitals with the same diagnosis. I envied her in there, so beautifully unreachable, at a time when anorexia wasn't such a cliché! How poetic!

But then I fell out of love with her, and with anorexia, though the latter was harder to shake, of course.

My classmate Caroline's love for Edie dwarfed mine. She arrived on campus with a short, platinum blond 'do, wearing a black leotard, feather-long false eyelashes, black tights, and dangly earrings. When she casually spouted off ideas that I knew were Edie's, I said nothing. *We all construct ourselves out of others,* I thought. But when Caroline mentioned that she, too, had been hospitalized at Silver Hill for anorexia, I couldn't resist trumping her with my connection stats.

"I was there, too, and also in Cornell, which used to

be called Bloomingdale. Edie was transferred there after she was at Silver Hill."

Caroline looked dismayed, but it didn't crack the façade. She already knew she was inheriting an icon blemished after years of being groped.

On YouTube, there are two thinspo videos that are montages of still photographs of Edie. The background music to one is Elliott Smith's song "Everybody Cares, Everybody Understands," which opens that way, followed by the line, "Yes, everybody cares about you / Yeah, and whether or not you want them to."

Foil

In the summer of 2004, Mary-Kate Olsen, famous twin, actress, and would-be fashion designer, publicly admitted that she was suffering from anorexia. More accurately, her managerial team (father included) revealed this to the media, as the mini-mogul, as she is often called, was mum on the subject and has pretty much remained so ever since. At the time, it was a well-circulated rumor that cocaine usage, not anorexia, was the main reason for her spindly frame, which is why her parents had her admitted to a facility better known as a drug rehab than an eating disorders clinic. A formerly bulimic and anorexic friend of mine built on this rumor and theorized that they chose to be open about her anorexia because it was the "more sympathetic" of the two, that if they said she had a drug problem, it would "look worse."

In any case, Mary-Kate's "nightmare," as *People* called it, was the feature article in every tabloid the week it came out, none of which failed to mention that she was also a fashion icon. In the following issue, her trip to rehab became one of the smaller boxes on the cover. Now the starlet was an emblematic figure for both budding anorexics and fashionistas. The heads of millions of teenage girls must have spun at the prospect of melding the two. Olsen continued to suffer from anorexia, or at least appear to, for the next few years. At one point over that period of time, I was in group therapy with a girl named Hanna, who was a sophomore at a prestigious private high school in New York City. She spent most of her time in group talking about her childhood friend Alexa, who attended the same school and was also anorexic. Other classmates, girls who knew of Hanna's eating disorder, would approach Hanna and say things like, "Alexa looks so sick" or "We have to do something to help Alexa!" This, of course, made Hanna feel like a terribly inferior anorexic. Alexa confided in Hanna every minute detail of her anorexia, probably both to unburden herself and to show off to someone who also used the same yardstick of achievement. At one point, Hanna began talking about how Alexa started dressing like Mary-Kate, donning slip dresses and cowboy boots and layers, layers, layers.

"People tell me I look like her. Do you think I look like her?" she would ask perfect strangers.

I had a dream in which I saw Mary-Kate Olsen at a party at what was then the Plaza Hotel in Manhattan. I saw her, and then someone I knew to be her ex-boyfriend reached out and touched my fingers in passing. He smiled at me. A fire drill went off in the hotel, and I called a friend of mine named Jackie, a fellow anorexic in real life, and told her that Mary-Kate Olsen was at this party.

"You have to follow her," she said. (When I relayed this dream to Jackie later on, she confirmed that this is exactly what she would have instructed me to do.)

I trailed Mary-Kate and a companion down the street until they parted and Mary-Kate boarded an escalator to nowhere. I got on the escalator beside hers and climbed a few steps so we were next to each other. She turned and looked at me and said in a friendly tone, "Do you think you would be so interested in me if I didn't have an eating disorder?"

"No," I answered softly. There was a moment of silence.

"So, what did you think?" Mary-Kate asked.

"What do you mean?" I said.

"My sickness. Did it look real?"

ANOTHER FOIL

She told me right away, to be fair to both of us. I went to see her for the first time my freshman year of college, when she was still in the dark office with the heavy red furniture on 86th Street. The decor was old-fashioned, and I liked that. In fact, it may have been why I chose her out of all the New York therapists I had "interviewed." At the end of the appointment, she dropped the bombshell. She told me about the cancer, about her prognosis, which was good, about her scheduling conflicts as a result of chemo. Temporary, she assured me.

I didn't think twice about it. Breast cancer is so prevalent and seemingly so treatable. Everyone I had ever known who had breast cancer had recovered. She said they caught it early. She said she would be fine.

Nine months passed. In this time, I was hospitalized twice; she continued chemotherapy. I went home for good. Her hair started to grow back into a chic, curly mop, and she lost a little of that pale chub I found so appealing, that layer of softness that comes with chemo. I, too, flourished despite small relapses and the occasional depressive episode. Our recoveries ran parallel to each other. We had survived together.

One session we discussed weight gain. I wanted her to tell me that it was possible to be happy with your weight even if it wasn't "perfect." I wanted her to cite herself as an example.

"I mean, I'm not entirely happy with my weight now. It irks me to look at pictures of myself from before . . . I gained weight because of chemo," she said.

I twitched at this comment. Who was she to be complaining to me about gaining weight? How dare she?

A year later she began to miss appointments more frequently. She would call and say she wasn't going to make it into the city that day. She wasn't feeling well. I was furious. I felt neglected, and I was just starting to recognize that I was falling back into old habits. The transition was slower and subtler than it had ever been before. By mid-July of

2004, between my sophomore and junior years of college, though, I couldn't deny some of the signs: the hours I spent at the grocery store only to emerge empty-handed, how I always volunteered to run down the five flights of stairs when friends visited, my roommate's sideways glance at me as I insisted that frozen yogurt was enough for dinner.

In moments of manic epiphany, I would think: *I'm going to die. What do I do?*

Please tell me what to do.

The night before I left on vacation with Maureen and her family, I called my therapist in a panic and left a voice message. How was I supposed to eat when faced with a table of not one but eight pairs of prying eyes? How could I consume what they made in restaurants, where they sautéed and garnished the food behind closed doors, where I couldn't see what they were adding to the pot? What do I do? *Tell me what to do.*

And a few hours later, her husband returned my call.

This, I suppose, was when I knew for certain that something was very, very wrong with her. She would never have crossed that line of therapeutic impropriety. I had seen her husband before, in fact. He was often reading a magazine in the waiting room of her office when I, the last appointment, exited. He looked like a burly computer programmer with his nerdy glasses and skin the color of putty. I asked her once if the man who was always in the waiting room was her husband, and she reluctantly said yes, he was. I asked if they had children.

"No, we haven't been able to." Her acceptance was

sad and wistful. It was the first time I had ever considered that she may have wanted a baby, and that her disease may have kept her from having one.

When Dr. K's husband called me, he told me to call Dr. W, who had been her mentor in graduate school and whom I had seen before while Dr. K was in treatment. I went to see Dr. W once and then absconded from the whole situation by failing to show up for appointments. My guilt, or "healthy self" as Dr. W would claim, got the better of me, though, and I started answering their calls. The three of us came to an arrangement: I would see Dr. W until Dr. K was well enough to start seeing me again.

But everything kept declining: my weight, my mood, my grasp of reality. I was convinced that Dr. W exaggerated how "bad" she thought I was so that I would admit myself to the hospital for some abstract reason based on principle or her own agenda. I called Dr. K and left a rambling message for her, begging her to assure me of Dr. W's credentials, her history. Would Dr. W lie to a malingerer like me? Did she even *know* I was a malingerer? Had my caveats been thorough enough? I didn't want to go back to the hospital. What good would it do, anyway? I had been three times before, and here I was, in some respects worse than ever. What was the point of any of this? I wanted Dr. K to evaluate me on her own and tell me it was okay. That I shouldn't be afraid. When she called me back, her voice was slurred, virtually unrecognizable.

"So many people are pulling for you," she said.

"Okay," I mumbled in response.

I felt the wind knocked out of me. The person on the other end of the line didn't sound like the doctor I had known for years. She sounded like a very sick person, someone hanging on by the tiniest of threads. She sounded drugged and weak, and here I was, calling and *begging* her to validate *my* illness. She told me that *she* was pulling for *me*.

How dare I.

When I was admitted to Cornell two months later, my second admission there, the doctor on call, who had an elongated face and Coke-bottle glasses, asked me often how I felt about Dr. K getting sick again. I would fix my eyes on walls the color of curdled milk and shake my head silently. I had retreated into a hovel of my own narcissistic making, and everything felt blank and cold. I knew there was grief in there, but the words wouldn't come out, and I didn't force them. It would be a few months until I felt anything at all, and when I finally had the strength and good sense to ask about Dr. K, I knew that there was only one question left to pose.

"She's going to die, isn't she?"

Dr. W looked at me lovingly and said, "I'm afraid she won't be with us for very much longer."

I was still only letting bits of feeling in through a hole in the dam, translating sadness over any little thing into despondency about my body, so my grieving was delayed. When it finally began in earnest, I nearly erupted. I found her obituary in the *New York Times*. "All who knew her will miss her dearly." Every time her husband's face became focused in my mind, I burst into tears. I became frantic over the fact that I didn't even know where she was buried, I couldn't even bring her flowers, I couldn't do anything at all for her. The psychoanalytic idea of transference perhaps played a role here—she had been a parental figure for me, as all my female therapists had, but I felt robbed of the chance to comfort her in her illness, as a daughter would do for an ailing mother. Her name was on the buzzer door of the office she and Dr. W had shared for at least a year after she passed. Every time I saw it, I winced. I wished I could buzz and go in and she'd be there in that big armchair, and I'd be able to say everything I hadn't gotten the chance to. I'd be able to say that I was sorry, and that I had loved her. I'd be able to say good-bye.

Over the years, when Dr. W would try to comfort me if she thought I was being too critical of myself, she would reference her own personality: her frequent tardiness, her bad habits—too much cream and sugar, always, in her coffee.

"I will never be one of those people who always shows up on time. Dr. K was one of those people. She was always punctual, ready, all her materials in order. She was perfect!" She laughed, it seemed, with genuine joy as she remembered her colleague and her friend.

I am not one of those naturally together people, either. I procrastinate and never balance my checkbook. I draw far-reaching conclusions based on few facts. Every piece of clothing I have is either torn or stained. I gossip and bite my fingernails and eschew important reading in favor of watching trashy television. I take all sorts of things for granted. I took Dr. K for granted, and I feel guilty about it.

If life were fair, and I could never have imagined how

anyone could argue against this, it would have been me who had died. *Should* have been. Dr. K would have continued to help people. She could have had a baby. I would have expired as a sickly child, instantly canonized, just as I had wanted. Sometimes I still believe that this is what should have happened, and I find myself arguing with God over his decisions even though I know it's hopeless. I have been given this thing called life that I know intellectually is so valuable and that I've toyed with for over a decade. She really wanted it, and even now, I'm not 100 percent sure that I do.

"Junkies and drunks," writes David Carr, "frequently end up putting a megaphone to their own pratfalls because they need to believe that all of the time they spent with their lips wrapped around glass, whether it was a bottle of vodka or a crack pipe, actually meant something."

I want it to mean something, the fact that Dr. K was my therapist, the fact that I chose her and then she was gone. I want her existence to have been sacrificed for mine, and for me to feel that heavy but empowering burden every minute of every day. I want there to be some corny and transcendental reason for all of this. And in fact I do believe that it *means something,* just that I will probably never know what that is, and this is yet another mystery with which I will have to live.

Minor Characters

When I reread *Prozac Nation* at twenty-five, I was, for lack of a less eloquent phrase, "grossed out" by Elizabeth Wurtzel's self-obsession. I patted myself on the back not only for avoiding such repulsive solipsism, but also for coming up with real, narrative-based proof of Wurtzel's narcissism (as opposed to just envying her success): throughout the entire book, began my critique, Wurtzel does not describe the physical attributes of any other characters. There are a few instances when she comments on the face of a one-night stand or the sad countenance of her mother, with whom she has a hopelessly entwined relationship, but never does she give due lip service to the appearances of the people around her. Whereas I, in contrast, paid serious attention to the people who scamper light-footed across my pages, talked about their button noses, their sideways smirks, their bones.

I thought this, of course, until an editor read my manuscript, and said to me, dismayed, "You do a great job describing the other patients in the hospital, and bringing them to life, but we don't get a sense of any of your life before that or outside of it. What about your parents, your family?"

I grimaced. Part of my motivation in leaving them out was literary—I wanted to avoid the typical memoir writer's pothole of going over every minute detail of his or her life as a child, everything his or her parents ever said. That wasn't what this book was about—it was meant to examine the way anorexia as an illness has changed as the world has, and the ways its veneer remains attractive to many people, particularly adolescent girls, despite the fact that its consequences are widely known. I also wanted the story, like I wanted myself, to exist in an ethereal midway point between dreams and consciousness. I wanted the child-me, who makes her appearance in the early pages, to be not more than a changeling, a magical creature who is most alive when seen from the outside by others, beguiled by her pixie spirit, and not as a regular kid who was on the swim team, good at spelling and bad at math, and had not one but two siblings, smart and capable parents, and a large extended family.

The last part of my motivation was a quick and fierce desire to protect them, particularly my nuclear family. I have always been terrified of their reaction to the finished product, whether or not they were included in it. Would they be terribly ashamed in front of their friends and colleagues, even if they know that they, too, have personal lives with baggage? Would they care that I was writing out of a desire to illuminate a subset of a problem that seemed to be adapting itself quickly to the modern age? Or would they interpret it as the prolonged and agonized misbehavior of *me,* the eternal adolescent, reaping for my own benefit the harvest of my pathetic past, which they finally thought was behind all of us?

The dilemma—talk about yourself with the hope it will do good for the world versus save face for the sake of your loved ones—felt particularly relevant a few weeks ago, when I met my father for a drink at a fancy after-work watering hole in midtown Manhattan. He was dressed in his work uniform—button-down light-blue shirt, ironed pants, messenger bag—and I in a green dress I save for interviews. It was humid, and the air dripped all over me. We welcomed the heavy air-conditioning in the crowded, noisy bar. I was discussing my life's plans with him, and he mentioned my book getting published. My father's personality is even keeled and not overly effusive, but I could see the telltale signs of pride bubbling to the surface, the trace of a smile he seemed to be trying to suppress. He is the one in my immediate family to whom I feel closest intellectually, the one who gets the most satisfaction out of my desire to blaze my own trail artistically. And yet as I sat there and watched his face low-beam with happiness, I felt crushed. Would this parental pride be null and void if he knew that I was dredging up painful things that didn't need to be unearthed for any of our sakes as individuals? Would he castigate me, or treat me differently, or disown me? What happens to those with whom you are closest when you lay yourself bare, almost entirely, for what you think, possibly naively, is the good of some distant other?

My brothers and I never talk about when I was sick, and we didn't much then, either. The older one once stumbled upon a draft of a suicide note I had writte, which he, in a panic, turned over to my mother, and would occasionally make snide comments about how I fed my dinner to our dogs most evenings, but these instances were rare. My parents brought them along sometimes to see me when I was in Silver Hill, but they didn't want my brothers to visit me at Cornell or Long Island Jewish, so instead we spoke on the phone. These conversations were infrequent and were mostly niceties, but occasionally something bigger poked through. One time, when I was talking to my brother from my bed at Schneider's, he asked hopefully, "Will you come home before you go back to school?" And it made me well up, because I hadn't believed he had really wanted me there.

Maybe, I thought later, the reason my family doesn't appear much in my writing is because my universe as an anorexic was, not surprisingly, very, very small, and my desire for a cultlike community closeness made it so that I only had room for those who shared my worldview. I was comfortable in hospitals and doctors' offices because the value system there was clearly the same as mine: the important things were weight, caloric intake, and whatever fell under the umbrella of "negative behavior." Everyone spoke the language of therapy, and there was little effort to force me to expand my horizons except in the simplest of ways. I sometimes pitied my parents and my extended family and the "normal" citizens of the world for having nothing extraordinary like anorexia to live for, but I knew deep down that the sense of superiority was ultimately born of cowardice. Their principles were more ambiguous and frightening to me. These included dignity, ethics, courage, and meaningful, not arbitrary, restraint. My family barely appears in these pages because they weren't the characters with the largest speaking parts at that point in time. As the director, I had to put them on the cutting-room floor, if I wanted to continue with my work, which, at the time, I did.

As I grew older—part of my recovery, I think, was due to sheer intellectual maturation—I found myself no longer wanting to play the role of sad, sad teenager, and so I moved from the smaller world of anorexia to the larger world of society. My life has not become easier, but my problems do seem on the whole more complex and fulfilling than they were when I was actively ill. I feel challenged positively, in a way that could even be important and occasionally selfless. My family, happily, is a major part of this new, real life. They are center stage, not waiting in the wings to be a part of it while a chorus of spindly girls and hospital staff plays out the familiar Greek tragedy before them. And I, I dance brazenly across the arena of their lives, too, present in body and mind for all these scenes I otherwise would certainly have missed.

FORESHADOWING

Freshman year of college: in group at Schneider's, Becky, the hospital employee who told me I might have a heart attack, had us write letters to ourselves that she said she would send us in six months. I carefully avoided the subject of health and behavior because I knew deep down that I would go back to my old habits with more experience and more fodder so I could lose weight. I wrote about my friends in the program, told myself not to forget them in their daily struggles. When we were done, we sealed them up and gave them to Becky. I never got that letter. As I wrote the straight chronology of my eating disorder later on, I wondered . . . what did that *mean*?

Or my junior year in college, when I moved into my dorm and found a ladybug lying belly up on my windowsill. *A dead ladybug*, I thought. *This is a bad omen.*

All these perceived symbols and auguries and oxymorons, I believed, pointed to the inevitability of my relapse(s) and, as an extension of this thought, my connection to the disease. It was written in the stars, something large and powerful enough to intrude even into another person's dream. There was a twisted-love-affair aspect to it that was comforting, an idea that this incomprehensible cosmic thing had "chosen" me akin to the way God chooses his martyrs. It made me feel—yes—special. *I am married to it,* I thought, *and in a sense, I always have been.* I think of the fatalistic line often spoken by addicts, "The first time I tried it, I was addicted." You are doomed before you begin.

Who needs foreshadowing when you have such preemptive certainty?

As I work even now to map out the plot of my life, I remain dismayed. Such literary structure called for a climax. Where was the plot's turning point? Where was the real heart attack, Greenfield's "emotional, narrative, and cinematic" tension? I remember a letter I received from an eating-disordered pen pal I met online early in my sick life, in which she expressed the belief that anorexia would make things exciting.

"I thought things would happen, and I just ended up sitting in my house all summer with a tube up my nose, playing cards with my sister, bored out of my skull."

I shuffled through the dull, gray, malnourished days and prayed, *Dear Lord, send me a deus ex machina,* for the moments that objectively ought to have felt like turning points didn't *feel* the way apogees should, even when I chanted, "This is really happening" over and over again as I was ushered through the familiar hospital admission routine. (*Later on you will try to convince yourself that it wasn't real, so try to remember,* I begged myself.) There was no white light, no chorus of angels. There was no real end. Anorexia, my violent husband, in the end gave me very little, and he was also cheating on me with thousands of other people all over the world. Best not to leave a note, then, not to have the knock-down, drag-out fight. Best to slip out at night unnoticed.

CHAPTER 12

THE END

"I'M HOPING," A PROMINENT NUTRITIONIST SAYS TO ME after reading my material, "that we can come up with some concrete solutions to these problems."

So am I. The appearance and growth of a phenomenon such as wannarexia, a desire for a devastating, potentially fatal illness, tells us that there must still be something profoundly wrong with the way we writers are presenting the subject. All this theorizing, all this eradication of stigma and spreading of awareness, and we are still instructing our youth how to starve, and we are making it look good. There are some obvious precautions parents can take: monitor what your children look at on the Internet, eat family dinners, keep lines of communication as open as possible, and if your child develops an eating disorder, encourage the sufferer to start therapy as soon as possible without rushing him or her into a hospital or group facility. Anorexics should be treated individually for as long as possible, or at least cared for by competent professionals in a general psych population as opposed to a strictly eating disorders unit. There has been, over the past decade, a decentralized effort to have psychiatric illness and addiction recognized as biochemical/ neurological problems at their core instead of being labeled moral failings or emotional weakness on the part of the sufferer. In the case of eating disorders, one positive consequence of framing the issue as biochemical, regardless of veracity, is that it begins to remove the romantic aura around the illness. And the more stringently anorexia is viewed and treated as a medical problem, the less we will enable the larger cultural romanticizing of it.

Country club rehabs with horseback riding and gourmet food and group trust falls, therefore, are mostly harmful. Treatment conditions shouldn't revert back to how they were in the days of Bedlam, but there is something hypocritical about loudly proclaiming anorexia an "illness" for which the sufferer cannot be held responsible (like cancer) and then making the treatment method look like a spa. Anorexia does have a psychiatric component where cancer does not, so the therapeutic needs of the patients must be filled; the medical component, however, ought to be as significant if not more so than the therapeutic one, especially considering that eating-disorder patients often need repeated reminders that they are damaging their bodies in serious, possibly lasting ways. A similar movement toward "medicalizing" has begun recently regarding addiction treatment, with many doctors decrying high-end rehab facilities, which lean heavily on twelve-step education and counsel by former addicts, as sorely lacking in technical expertise. Rehabs, treatment centers, and hospitals should ultimately not be comfortable places, and one shouldn't linger in them for longer than necessary. The idea is to *not* want to return.

I'm a proponent of the Maudsley method, which teaches parents and siblings to be actively involved in the anorexic's treatment by supervising all meals and snacks. The Maudsley method, also called the Maudsley approach, was developed in the late 1970s at the Institute for Psychiatry, a division of the famous Maudsley Hospital in London. Rather than send an anorexic off to break bread with other anorexics, the Maudsley method advocates that the sufferer eat all meals and snacks with his or her family. If the anorexic does not finish the prescribed amount of food, there are consequences that resemble traditional punishments given to children, such as revoking television or phone privileges, or not allowing the anorexic to go to a friend's house or a party. The family—the Maudsley definition does not limit the family to the nuclear one—meets with a supervising therapist once a week, and the patient, in addition to this, undergoes psychiatric treatment and regular physical examinations. There are, of course, limitations to the treatment— it's difficult to provide round-the-clock care for one's child when there is a financial need for one or both parents to work, and older patients, who may have suffered longer, tend to be less sensitive to their parents' interference in their treatment than their adolescent counterparts—but overall it's a methodology that deserves much more attention and study.

Other solutions are more theory based and mostly verbal. As Caroline Knapp put it in *Appetites*, "Even the smallest steps toward change involve linguistic shifts, gateways marked with nouns and verbs." In other words: how can we present and discuss anorexia more effectively? How can we adjust our language?

Most obviously, and this falls under the category of "a prescription for culture": when writing about eating disorders in general, do not include details of the sick person's intake and dieting techniques. Do not include the person's weight statistics.

Angela Ross was fourteen when she began trolling pro-ana sites for tips on how to drop weight quickly. By college, she had come to see the horror in them, and she started a group on Facebook called "Stop Pro-Ana!" that was influential in the social media giant's decision to ban the sites from their server. The argument that ultimately won out over those who cried First Amendment was that pro-ana sites were no different in essence from web pages like Catching the Train, a social group for people who wanted to commit suicide and needed encouragement. Ross, who has been interviewed about her efforts in major print publications, states that "going through this and being interviewed, [the reporters] were more concerned about how much weight I had lost and in what amount of time." I told her, in response, how a few years earlier, I had read an interview with a young sitcom actress who had recently overcome anorexia.

The reporter asked her what her lowest weight was, and she responded that she didn't think it appropriate to say, because it might "trigger" people reading the piece, or in any case wouldn't add anything. I was impressed by the actress's steadfast intelligence and her meta-awareness.

A year later, I read another interview with the same actress. This time, when the reporter asked what her lowest weight was, she told him. My first thought? She probably just broke down.

Rx, for both parties: Just *stop*.

Many of the books I have re-read in the process of my research are great: powerfully written, beautifully worded, and rife with insight. The tones are full of conviction, intelligence, and honesty, which is why I chide authors for then including their once-upon-a-deathly-time daily calorie allotments or exercise routines or lowest weights. Many explicitly express intimate knowledge of the perversely competitive strain of anorexia; some are even familiar with the community-based aspects of eating disorders in modern cultures, as everyone from teens looking to diet to full-blown anorexics seek to expand their behavioral repertoire through reading and swapping stories.

To destroy anorexia, we must devalue its currency. We must refuse to speak its language, to play its game. Leave the salacious and profitable details for the medical professionals. By doing this, we cut anorexia's legs from beneath it. This steadfast stance is no less than a subversive act.

There are three easy ways to change the dialogue. The first is that we need to stop touting the anorexic population as misunderstood. Surely as individuals they often are, but as far as the general myths go, we need to figure out precisely which ones to debunk. The most popular myth has always been the characterization of anorexics as white, upper-middle-class, and female. A *Newsweek* article from September 2008 lauded the release of the book *Going Hungry*. The *Newsweek* writer's tagline was "Anorexics can be male, old, Latino, black, or pregnant." But doctors and researchers made this same statement almost two decades ago, when studies in the early 1990s showed that 10 percent of the anorexic population was male. The inimitable trauma peddler Oprah Winfrey had male anorexics on her show back in 1996. The authors of *Going Hungry* were, therefore, rehashing this statistic and pretending it was new. The writer of the glowing *Newsweek* article eventually concedes that "of the 10 million women and 1 million men who do cope with anorexia and bulimia in this country, it is true that the majority of those documented are white." Her subtext is resentful. She senses that perhaps this is not the myth we need to "debunk," the grave assumption about anorexics we must attack. Wouldn't it be nice if this was all that was wrong? It is, after all, much easier to champion a population, especially one that is visibly feeble, than it is to seemingly critique it.

Perhaps what we need to do is actually *restore* some of the myths about anorexia, namely, that it's a problem of vanity, or resurrect some of the stigma that surrounds it, in hopes that we move away from radically accepting it.

In *Going Hungry,* editor Kate Taylor tries to dispel the

idea of the anorexic as vapid model or ballerina types pathetically obsessed with appearance. But I can only think of one book in which the anorexic is portrayed this way, *The Best Little Girl in the World*, and it was originally published in 1978, a good thirty years before Taylor took up the hammer to destroy the image of Steven Levenkron's Kessa. Myriad books on anorexia, and the gross mischaracterization of its sufferers, have been published in that interim. So much effort has been expended to save the anorexic from ridicule, to lift his or her image from the depths of silliness, that one can't help but wonder if perhaps we're raising it too high. When, exactly, do we cross the line from condemning the victims to canonizing them?

Before I read *Going Hungry*, I made a mistake: I read the *New York Times* review of it. The analysis put forth by Ginia Bellafante is razor-sharp, astute, and articulate, and nails Taylor's major problem right on the head. My opinion seems to be dwarfed by hers. I am very much indebted to it. She writes:

> To read *Going Hungry* is to suspect an effort has been made to convince us there is no such thing as a superficial anorexic, no creature whose radical self-regulation comes unaccompanied by an impressive imagination or intelligence . . . [Taylor] has emphatically reproduced one of the most prevailing stereotypes of all—the anorexic as achiever or genius.

By collecting eighteen writers, including a Pulitzer Prize winner and numerous Ivy League graduates, to write about their experiences, which they do beautifully, Taylor is perpetuating a big problem. She is supporting the idea that anorexia leads to a type of fame—or at least bragging rights—but she does a big disservice to readers by neglecting to include just one "civilian" voice, such as a person without a Pulitzer, maybe, or someone whose life was essentially decimated by anorexia. (One contributor struggles with infertility, and in selecting this piece, Taylor made probably her best curatorial decision.) She writes in her introduction, "The kind of person who develops anorexia is driven equally by a desire to be accepted and a desire to feel special and distinct, a hunger for praise and a hunger for self-expression." It seems counterintuitive, then, to present the reader with eighteen examples of people who seem to have achieved exactly that, not really *in spite of* their eating disorders but *because of them,* or at least because of the personality traits that led them toward anorexia in the first place. This romanticized view of the illness as a manifestation of "impressive imagination or intelligence" is a big part of what attracted me, and while it may not directly be the bait that caught most of the other squirming little fish, it certainly will do nothing but inhibit their escape from the labyrinth of sick logic.

The second thing we need to do is try to cut the perceived link between genius and madness. I can attest to the fact that there are most definitely superficial anorexics out there, ones who possess a paltry understanding of what the word *imagination* even means. Sometimes the ignorance is sweet, a puerile brain overtaken by a disease that belies the organ's innocence or its youth. Sometimes it is archetypal, belonging to a vacuous model or a disciplined, doltish athlete. Stereotypes do exist in abundance, in fact, and after all, is it any more difficult to believe this than it is to believe that most of the approximately eight million individuals who suffer from anorexia in this country are really just misguided geniuses?

There are documented cases of anorexia in people who were also mentally handicapped. A fifteen-year-old with an IQ of 62 was the subject of an article published in 1979, and a thirty-five-year-old woman with Down syndrome was the focus of another published in 1984. In the latter case, the onset of the disease was attributed largely to the late mental and physical development. The subject was wrestling with teenage issues of identity and sexual maturation, and communicated the anxiety surrounding this process in the simplest, basest terms she could manage: through behavior with food. The most frightening cases of anorexia I've ever seen are those in children, whose brains are not developed enough to deal with such a formidable enemy. I was hospitalized with a number of kids ages ten to twelve, and it was heartbreaking and disturbing that they could not comprehend their cunning malady. They were much more capable of being willful and ignorant than those of us a bit older. Eleven-year-old Adena was the perfect defiant anorexic, letting her Ensure dribble from her mouth onto her hands and smearing it all over the cup to avoid drinking it. She wasn't underweight at all, and even had baby fat, but she was viewed as a particularly troublesome case for the doctors because she behaved basically like a bratty toddler. Therapists didn't make her—or the other patients under thirteen—participate in groups because they figured the jargon would just go above their heads. Adena was a Hasidic Jew, and there was another patient there who was, too, and after feedings every day, Adena would slink into the dining room and taunt the other girl in Yiddish, demanding to know if she had consumed her Ensure and bragging that she had let most of hers spill onto the floor. In the mornings before we got weighed, Adena would run around naked and slap at her doughy body, saying, "I'm hot, I'm hot! It's all this fat on my body!"

Finally she was consuming so little that they gave her the tube and so much Thorazine that she passed out every five minutes. When she was discharged, though, she walked out the front door with that same blank, careless stare she always wore. That expression—her soulless signature—haunts me still.

The most unsettling case of anorexia I've ever come across was one I encountered during my early web-surfing days. A worried father posted an essay about his sick daughter, who, at nine, had viewed a kids' news program on Nickelodeon that featured a segment on anorexia. The show focused specifically on one young girl who was very ill, and showed the skeletal subject in various states of undress. Shortly after viewing the program, the man's daughter began to cut back on her food intake. Before long, she was so malnourished she had to be hospitalized. When her father asked her why she had started dieting, she replied that after having seen the Nickelodeon show, she thought that she should be careful not to get fat so that she would never have to become anorexic and risk looking like the terribly ill girl featured on Nickelodeon.

Anorexia is a viral monstrosity: no one is safe. There are quasi-geniuses who develop anorexia, yes, preternaturally gifted musicians and the uncannily perceptive, etc., but there are also teenagers, stereotypical models and ballerinas, vapid, unlovable people, witless children, and, *gasp,* the utterly average. The disease is Bobby Fischer playing chess, and it doesn't care if its opponent is lacking in strategic knowledge. It relishes an ill-equipped adversary.

We make anorexia desirable by connecting it to brilliance, and also by talking about it poetically, by making it something that enhances a person's aura, makes them more glamorous. Marya Hornbacher's stated intent in *Wasted* was to deglamorize the problem, but as she became a pro-ana icon, it's safe to say she glamorized it in a darker and more dangerous way. It was an early attempt, though not much by way of marring the image of anorexia seems to have been done since *Wasted* was published in 1998. The writers of *Going Hungry,* published a decade later, could have made a few more efforts in that direction. For example, they could have spared the reader any in-depth description of the anorexic body, especially when it sounds lovely and graceful. "[When I was anorexic,] my older brother's friend took some photographs of me . . . My eyes look big and dreamy; my lips are full. I have a slender body, long legs," writes Francesca Lia Block. She uses the metaphor of "faeries" throughout her piece, likening them to anorexia itself. "That perfect blend of angelic and demonic—the faerie. Ethereal, delicate, able to fly. Also dangerously seductive, beckoning us into worlds unknown." Beautiful writing; great *advertising*. Seems as if anorexia endows the sufferer with a certain tenebrous, ascetic glow, an air of lithe detachment, something that many writers in the book cop to having wanted prior to the onset of their illness (low self-esteem is very fashionable). Jennifer Egan fantasizes about being "irresistible, strong." Sarah Haight envied a dancer who seemed, from the outside, "vaguely detached, cool." Joyce Maynard yearns to look "fragile." These things mean thin, and being thin means getting love/admiration, and all was seemingly achieved.

Going Hungry is peppered with tenuous connections between the anorexic body and objects or characters of perfect, tight, "detached" beauty: the faeries, for one; also images of the emaciated Christ, weeping on the cross; Saint Joan of Arc (as portrayed by the "gamine" Jean Seberg); Degas's ballerinas; Hemingway in his prolific Parisian period; the perfect geometric circle; "a snow white princess who glided along in a winter fairytale, leaving no footprints." Most of the writers still seem attached to these ideas of beauty, some because they rely on them so heavily as literary imagery and others because they admit they still covet the waif as idea and image. To be fair, the subtitle is *Writers on Desire, Self-Denial, and Overcoming Anorexia*. How can a writer endeavor to write something *unappealing*? Or worse, downright ugly? Is it possible to do that without rendering the product—in this case, the book—entirely undesirable, something no one wants to read at all?

And in all this lies the third problem with how anorexia has historically been discussed: those doing so have always recovered, and while it is important to inspire hope in those suffering, it is also important to remind them, and everyone else, that sometimes people don't get better, that sometimes what is lost is more than what is gained, that sometimes the struggle really is for naught. And even if one does rise like the phoenix from tragedy, the ashes of what was still scatter the ground and can never be retrieved. Ernest Becker, the preeminent cultural anthropologist who wrote the seminal book *The Denial of Death*, captures this perfectly when he expands upon the wisdom of German psychiatrist Frederick Perls. "As Perls put it, 'To suffer one's death and to be reborn is not easy.' And it is not easy precisely because so much of one has to die."

In *Going Hungry*, almost every single essay has an exculpatory undertone, as if each writer is confirming his or her anorexia as a legitimate attempt at self-improvement. They don't delineate how the anorexia *failed* them and how it, in fact, may have destroyed some of their potential as opposed to awakening it. Marya Hornbacher is guilty of this, too. She writes in a 2006 follow-up section to the book entitled "P.S." that "struggle doesn't frighten me anymore because I know I will survive." Somehow anorexia becomes something that is seen as *hastening* emotional growth, encouraging it, in the long run.

This refrigerator magnet aphorism grates on me because I think that struggling with anorexia or bulimia actually does the exact *opposite;* it stunts emotional and intellectual growth and in doing so renders one less capable of navigating the emotional maze we call day-to-day life. Those who survive inhabit bodies that have been sometimes irrevocably damaged by starvation. Our bones are brittle; our hearts wheeze. While you're absent from school, insulated from real life by the chilly buzz of malnutrition, stuck in one place and one routine and one meal plan, on a metaphorical treadmill, your contemporaries are growing socially, physically, and emotionally. You remain still; they move forward. I'm still recovering in this way, even though I have next to no anxiety about food anymore. I still have to tell myself that it's okay to be touched in the most platonic of ways. At the sign of a major obstacle ahead, I sometimes make elaborate plans to fast until I collapse and someone picks me up and swaddles me in a baby blanket. So no, I don't think I am stronger as a result of my struggle. The normal processes of physical *and* emotional maturation were compromised. My bones and my brain and my heart (the romantic one and the physical one) are weaker than they would have been had I never developed anorexia, and while I can help them to grow now, nurture what is left, they will never be as strong as they could have been. I believe this wholeheartedly, and this belief is the crux of why I don't relapse. Following the no-pain-no-gain logic, you could just struggle and struggle and struggle until you reach near-superhuman status. When would the levee break, eventually?

"I will survive this"—something about it sounds passive, and sad, and scripted.

"What *Wasted* taught me was that it was possible to be sort of sick," Jackie, my friend who told me to follow Mary-Kate Olsen in my dream, said over dinner one evening. "And that's what 'sort of sick' looked like, and so it was okay to be that way."

In the last little vignette of *Wasted,* Hornbacher doesn't sound *sort of sick,* but like someone who is still *very* sick. In the course of a paragraph, she weighs herself and notes that she has lost weight. She jumps on a treadmill and then passes out in the shower. Many of the contributors to *Going Hungry,* too, give examples of how they have not completely recovered from their eating disorders. They seem to have held on to small, benign things: a desire to isolate themselves, an intense self-discipline, a borderline-naturally slim figure. They're still a *little* anorexic. And these things, dare I say it, are sort of enviable attributes, ones that actually may be more beneficial than not. The authors have remained just ill enough, just controlled enough, to cultivate their creativity, keep their senses heightened, maintain a figure that is svelte but healthy enough to function, have babies, have relationships, get educations, make money. Win Pulitzers. At least Hornbacher had the decency to point out her permanent medical consequences. When a person ends up thin, published, and decorated with awards, the narrative ends up as a strict and formulaic redemption narrative with a skinny protagonist. Condensing the story into a "triumph over an obstacle" narrative is to simplify it to a worrisome degree, and to confirm to a young, confused person that you can have your disease and survive it, too—without permanent scars. It is to state that to have had it and overcome it is to have done something remarkable.

It is very difficult to recover, but remarkable it is not. Approximately 90 percent of people who suffer do it. What would be really remarkable is remaining healthy in a world in which one is essentially handed opportunities or manuals for self-sabotage, a world in which acts of histrionic self-destruction are, in many cases and in many ways, considered more extraordinary and more worthy of attention than keeping your head above the surface of the water, than living gently and quietly. Remarkable is enforcing clarity of mind when the world around you tells you that everything is *complicated* and nothing that is not so is worth anyone's time. A memoir of a person who, in this era, made it to the age of thirty without being diagnosed with a psychological disorder or struggling with an addiction: now *that* would be remarkable.

The koan-like conclusions of these writers—"Struggle makes you stronger"— brings us back to the fundamental issue of language, and how to use it properly when we talk about anorexia. One tactic might be the potentially aggravating Zen concept of focused ignorance. We have to at once address the anorexia doggedly and at the same time brush it aside as the least important characteristic of the individual suffering from it. Anorexia, as I've said, endows the sufferer with a sense of uniqueness, a feeling of being chosen. It is essential to treat the disease without in any way reinforcing anorexia's snide assertion *I am the only thing worthwhile about you.* We do this by changing our language, by maintaining a formality in our treatment system, by asserting control over our own narratives, and finally, in a Buddhist way, by understanding that these narratives are not really *ours* at all, but everyone's. Let go of the individual as the center. Instill in them the dual Hasidic wisdom that for their sake, the world was created, but also, they are dust and ashes.

If we fail to do this, we have enabled a system in which a person can easily continue to believe that his or her transgressions are to be cultivated, written about, and celebrated. When your greatest source of inspiration has been your problem all along, and the public thirsts for a new story, you do as Marya Hornbacher and Elizabeth Wurtzel did: move down your records to the next diagnosis and write a memoir about your new problem. Kayla, a pen pal of mine who is far more eloquent than I am, wrote me upon reading a blurb about Hornbacher's third book, *Madness,* in an issue of *People:*

A few weeks ago I picked up *People* upon seeing the "Britney's Mental Illness" cover, and inside they had a little box with Marya Hornbacher talking about her new memoir on bipolar. My first thought was, ANOTHER memoir? What an attention whore! How self-involved! But I got to wondering about how much one can stretch this out, this talking (and writing) about oneself and one's problems. Maybe it's not that I have so much to talk about, maybe the cause is actually the effect: I have such desire to dialogue with an audience, to shape my life into a story and have this product, that I make sure (sometimes subconsciously, sometimes less so) that there are lots of issues to be exploited for their artistic potential.

At what point does self-examination become a cannibalistic activity? When does it just serve as a method of procrastination or justification? Does society enable these attention-seeking cycles? (Of course.) Dialogue and story are universal desires, but if the dialogue begins with anorexia, the anorexic, typically a person who craves above all else clarity and identification, might believe that the illness and/or its accompanying bad habits (cutting, alcohol consumption, over-exercise) is the only thing about him or her that is dialogue-worthy. Therapy can sometimes allow these ideas to fester; it can actually confirm the hypothesis that what is special is my Problem. Making one's story something easily consumed by everyone, something that can be lauded and gawked at and loved, is an extension of this idea.

Recently, I struck up a bit of a conversation via e-mail with Hornbacher. My image of her as haughty about her eating disorder and her writing career officially crumbled as I found her to be kind, responsive, and intelligent. This was somewhat to my chagrin. It would have been easier to continue to resent her than to embrace my ambivalence toward her and her writing. Her honesty inspired me: she expressed trepidation at the way *Wasted* was interpreted by the young people who coopted it as a didactic text, and wondered if perhaps she was too young to have so publicly lamented her struggles. She also shared many of my views about eating disorders, most notably that it may not be best to label people as "always recovering." She has, she told me, nearly twenty years of recovery under her belt, and describes herself as at peace. Like Hornbacher, I am loath to describe myself as "always struggling." I prefer to imagine myself as stomping away from my illness, abandoning it to fester alone, like an infectious disease without a host organism. To quote Emily Dickinson via Hornbacher, "There is, in the end, the letting go." Or, to paraphrase Brigitte Bardot, a female role model whose shape I prefer: "I leave before being left. I decide."

• • •

"I'M WONDERING," BRIAN, A FELLOW WRITER, ASKS DURING a workshop one day, "if you had any real relationships during this time? In this piece, everything is so sinister. Everyone has these ulterior motives. These kids are going through this terrible ordeal and they feel alone. Did you experience any moments of tenderness?"

Christmas season of 2002 I spent at Schneider Children's Hospital. The lot of us passed our mornings wrapping gifts for the children on the unit with cancer and diabetes and broken arms. We did Secret Santas within our program. I don't remember who I had or what I got them, but I do remember that Faye had Roberta. Roberta was pale and had long, greasy brown hair. She went to a boarding school upstate but had to leave when she became sick. This was not her first time on the Schneider's-Cornell merry-go-round. She rarely spoke, but when she did her voice was surprisingly deep. When it was her turn to receive her gift, she took the shoe box from Faye's hands and opened it. A spontaneous smile burst across her face.

"I didn't get to a thousand, but in Korean culture, they're good luck," Faye said.

Inside the box were what seemed to be more than a thousand tiny paper cranes of all colors. We crowded around and gazed in awe at Faye's meticulous handiwork, the product of her heart.

Roberta said over and over again, "I can't believe you did this."

After that, we all started making little paper cranes when we were bored, which was often. Our fingers furiously folded the tiny sheets of patterned origami paper. Little birds littered the dayroom, wedged themselves between the crevices in the couch, lined the edges of the tables where we sat and ate our snacks.

This is our cry. This is our prayer. Peace in the world.

These are good people, mostly, beneath the hardened, ugly shell of anorexia. These are lovely young women, boys, men, grandmothers, sisters. You can feel this sometimes in the hospital, real humanity poking through, when someone holds your hand, when a friend makes you a birthday card, decorates it with her minuscule handwriting and equally miniature pictures of balloons and confetti. But this is a tenderness *in spite of,* one that we had to fight for, one that, many times, was second-guessed by a brain and a soul still deeply involved in, even enamored of, the illness.

Is she happy I'm being discharged because it means I

am at my goal weight now, which means I am better *(worse)?*

The unadulterated capacity for tenderness comes only with time, perhaps, distance and age and restful nights, hearty meals, travels. It is only real when you can feel it for yourself, a nauseating therapy cliché that is, not shockingly, quite valid. The less you feel that pang of jealousy when you hear that someone is "struggling," the closer you are to knowing what it is to feel free of anorexia's narcotic influence. I heard that Lily Brown was struggling and I felt terrible for her, and only a smidgen jealous. When I learned that she had taken the initiative and insisted on being hospitalized and, afterward, regained strength and enrolled in college, I was happy that she might finally be able to experience a little bit of that elusive "real life." Since before puberty, she had been completely engrossed in her illness, and now she might be able to do what a nineteen-year-old girl ought to be doing. She could drink beer and eat pizza at three in the morning. She could sneak into bars before she was twenty-one. She could fool around with a boy. She could have real friends. All these things seem to me, at this point, far more worthwhile, even in terms of character building, than any of the dramatic close calls or meltdowns or hospitalizations. Any of the *hard times*.

Once, Mariah, who had caused such angst for my friend Orah, called me after having dinner with a mutual acquaintance. "I'm doing really well!" she said. I was happy for her, *really* happy, not just happy because of what that meant *for me* or my sense of self. I had known her as a child close to death. She had once shoved chunks of an orange down her throat in an attempt to finish a meal on time. Because her stomach was so tiny, each piece rose involuntarily, and she caught the regurgitated orange mush in her cupped hands while tears streamed down her face. She had wanted to be able to "move up a level" so she could take walks on the hospital grounds. No one had the heart to tell her that not one of the patients present had ever been taken on a walk despite his or her ranking. The nurses were never available, or perhaps willing, to accompany us. After the meal, only partially digested, she lay on her back on the couch, wheezing and weeping in pain. Now she was eating out in a restaurant, taking normal bites of chicken and salad and buttering her bread and holding conversation during it all.

"I love you!" she said. Her voice was still squeaky and childish, but her statement was firm and unabashed.

"I love you, too," I responded.

I bumped into characters from my hospital life in the real world sometimes. Lisa in Bloomingdale's, engaging in retail therapy post-breakup. She looked sad, but it was her sadness, and not the anorexia's. Out of the blue, Laura wrote me an e-mail announcing that she was engaged. Liz and I write often, and she tells me about graduate school and the cross-country road trip she has planned to gather data for her thesis in urban planning and architectural preservation.

And Orah and I finally find a time to meet up. We don't get to do any of the things we had planned, like learn to skateboard or go see the movies under the Brooklyn Bridge, but we manage to meet at a Barnes & Noble near her therapist's office. She is a grown woman now, though I can still see the faint outline of the child's face I remember within her new, fuller one. No more blue-tinted chapped lips; a stronger voice, but still the slightest lisp. I have never seen anyone look so beautiful. She's just started her freshman year of college and is unsure of what she wants to study. And as we're walking through the Times Square subway station, she mentions taking anthropology, reading the texts, and finding it fascinating. There are so many possible things to be, she muses, and yet we're all made up of the same matter. Why are we who we are? How can we bridge the gaps and learn to talk to one another despite our vast differences? We pass by an older Latin American man playing a keyboard adorned with mechanical dancing dolls.

"Like me and this fellow here . . ." Orah says. "We're so similar, but I can't do that."

And my heart fills instantly. She wonders. Genuine curiosity is anorexia's arch nemesis; it nudges you outside of yourself, whereas anorexia is only interested in making you curl inward, rubbing the edges of your Self until your fingertips bleed. Orah looks around at the people bustling through the station with an openness and warmth that could never be cultivated in the belly of the beast. This respectful fulfillment of her own inquisitive desires is her ticket to moving forward.

She will be okay.

• • •

WHEN I WAS HOSPITALIZED AT SILVER HILL IN 1999, THERE WAS a therapist who loved aphorisms. One of her favorites was that we should never forget how sick we were, because if we did, we would think it was okay to do again.

This idea struck me as somewhat backward. How does clinging to the memory of a past love help us in letting it go? Isn't remembering bound to lead to nostalgia, the greatest and most perverted romanticism? The more we tried to conjure up how our anorexia made us feel, wouldn't it just make us ache to feel that way again? Yearn not for some paltry, halfway experience of it, but for the *real* one, which is just a choice to make, one we always know we have?

Or maybe we'll understand it, then, when it's crystallized in memory? The illness itself, and how we got it? When we can analyze it, like a text? It's clear why Sylvia Plath's fictional foil Esther Greenwood tried to kill herself. I can find the paragraph in which Kessa has reached the point of no return. I can tell by the structure of her sentence here. I get it now. But real life is not a book, and even memories morph into something new as time passes. As Freud wrote, "A thing which has not been understood inevitably reappears; like an unlaid ghost, it cannot rest until the mystery has been solved and the spell broken."

But maybe, in the case of such a baffling and cruel disease, it won't be made clear. The spell will never be broken. Maybe every time we call forth its memory, through restricting "just one more day" or revisiting hospitals or reading memoirs or "telling our stories," we'll learn what we've feared all along: that there is no clear-cut answer, that it never has and never will make sense, and to dive deeper into it is to gaze further into Nietzsche's abyss, which, the philosopher said, will just stare right back into the abyss of you.

Of course we all want to remember parts of the journey down below, just for sentiment's sake. To keep little things, like a mental image of a friend's pin-thin ankles, white as Dove soap. Repeat anecdotes to a loved one. We write poems about the hospital, essays, books. We wear our ID bracelets, all of them, even after we have been discharged. I even saw the venerable Lily Brown, who could want for nothing, try to sneak a robe from Cornell the day of her discharge.

It's okay to remember, sometimes . . . But forgetting? This is harder, and with anorexia, I believe, it's what is necessary. In his book *The Botany of Desire,* Michael Pollan theorizes about why a plant like marijuana, known to deteriorate the memory, would be popular given that people as a whole are so fearful of memory loss. Marijuana, according to the scientists Pollan consulted, acts like cannabinoids, which are chemicals occurring naturally in the brain specifically designed to inhibit the process of making memories. Pollan rescues the act of forgetting, usually denigrated as a failing of the human brain, and reminds us that it is indeed a neurological *act.*

"Much depends upon forgetting," he closes.

And so I let myself forget. First, selfishly, I let myself remember: I remember when they took Tom to Acute Care for throwing a chair in a family meeting, and he came back wearing all white, and I gasped, thinking of people whose hair turns white after a traumatic event. I remember Jenny at the piano, pressing a few solitary notes, the way they hung in the dead, dusty air. I remember Coco's sunken temples pulsing and contracting as she sobbed and gritted her teeth and said, "I want to throw up!" And middle-aged religious fanatic Marie moaning through the night that she was dying, and how in the morning, when we had to line up for the bathroom, she was drooling, passed out in restraints on a gurney lifted above the ground and angled just enough to be reminiscent of a crucifix. The nurse on duty flipped through a magazine listlessly, and hours later Marie was gone. My hand with the IV in it, bloated and cold like a dead fish, useless on New Year's Day. The row of bony asses in the shower; Adrienne's zombie face post-ECT; me, in a dream, the skin of my chest pinned back, electrodes stuck into my heart. My wispy plea, even in sleep, "Don't waste your money on me. I'm not *that* bad."

Suddenly, I want to tell you everything I remember. I want to show you all the things I've kept, the worksheets and the farewell notes written in microscopic handwriting, maybe drive you by one of the facilities, point to where I slept, the tiny light in the night. I'll show you the cigarette burns near my wrist, almost completely faded, and tell you why and how I did each one. I want to, but I won't. I'm letting go. I'm actually doing it, right now, right this second. There is a pang of terror, still. Who will I be if I let go of my past? Confronted, naked, with this endless steppe of time, my future?

But then I remember Nietzsche: "The future influences the present as much as the past."

I write my future and there is no anorexia in it. I accept all the ramifications of my signature. I have to let go in order to move back to Paris and decorate my apartment with dried flowers and eat eggs every morning and have a baby. Is that my plan, or someone else's?

"There are many things to do," Hornbacher wrote. "There are books to write and naps to take. There are movies to see and scrambled eggs to eat."

Is this the moment when everything makes sense, or did I miss it? If so, when was that? When I broke my foot walking down the stairs and felt for a few days how fragile my body is, my bones were? On my trip to Paris when I ate baguettes for two months and realized how amazing it can feel to have fat on you, real flesh you can grab and touch and know? When I encountered the shivering, infamous neighborhood drug addict on the street who begged me to buy her a Vitamin Water?

"I'm bulimic," she says. "Tell me honestly . . . do you think I'm fat?"

Her face brightens when I mention Cornell. "I was there!" she exclaims.

Is it when I envision her running through the hallways, hear Janine telling her to *sit down?* Do I connect those two images? Does Sara the bulimic-turned-crack-addict make it all come together? Is she the literary foil who will make me see myself, and my story, for what it is: both dramatic and disjointed, unique and universal?

No, she isn't.

Or is it when I relapse, again, and when I write what I think is an epiphany on an index card and tape it to my refrigerator. "Chewing makes me feel like an animal." I stare in the mirror and swing my arms and am fifteen again in the handicapped bathroom, watching my bones undulate beneath the pale skin on my chest.

No. Definitely not then.

But not when I weep, either, at the shame of being twenty-four and still unable to really *understand*, to really *let go*. Not when I take laxatives just-one-more-time or when I reluctantly sip my Ensure or later when I decide that yes, I will have dessert, or when my mother tells me for the first time, "We will get through this . . . together."

Is it when I finish this book?

It must be in the near future, that elusive *soon* when I start to believe my boss's assertion that "you *can* overcome your issues overnight," when I catch someone staring at me and think it must be just *because,* when in my dreams I wander through the hospital grounds and find that it's simply dead quiet among the wan hedges and expansive, browning lawns. Without question the end will be when I run into Claudia and Annalise and Jenna and they are full-faced and smiling and they join hands with the seventh-grade girls from the nurse's office and Adrienne and Ruby and Lily Brown and my brothers and Kerry and Mary-Kate Olsen and Jackie and Marya Hornbacher and Angela Ross and Jennifer the clumsy spaghetti eater and the specter of Vali Myers and lovely little Orah, and they all dance ecstatically around the edifice, which is halfway built, surely.

This is the end of the story.

ACKNOWLEDGMENTS

In addition to the many people whose writings I cite here, there are others who contributed in ways big and small to the writing of this book. First off, I need to thank those who agreed to be interviewed or have their words, long-ago forgotten, rephrased by me. This list includes, but perhaps isn't limited to, Sara Shaw née Hilton, Laura Moffett, Kerry McAuliffe, Jacqueline Marino, Elizabeth Boyle, Tomas Vengris, Marisa Harary Zucker, Adam Davies, Lauren Edelman, Kate Lieberman, and Angela Ross. Thanks to Brian Mockenhaupt, also, for allowing me to glean a bit off a wonderful essay of his, and to Daphne Merkin, Naomi Wolf, Joan Jacobs Brumberg, and Marya Hornbacher, for giving me personal permission to excerpt a little more than a bit of their work. Thanks also to those who, via their agent, estate, or publisher, also allowed themselves to be quoted

For a thorough read and a speedy analysis, I'm indebted to Hannah Sheldon-Dean; for professional clarification, to Rebecca Abbott and Drs. Rebecka Peebles and Monica Sethi; and for reliable advice related to publishing and writing, to Russ Beck, Carrie Hagen, Sarah Burningham, Nemira Gasiunas and Matt Bialer. Every writer needs a business-savvy advocate, and mine is Lauren Smythe at InkWell Management. Her enthusiasm for this projects, and her knowledge of writing as a business and an art form, is unparalleled.

I wouldn't be half the writer I am today without the wonderful MFA program at Goucher College, particularly my insanely talented mentors, Suzannah Lessard, Dick Todd, Diana Hume-George, and Leslie Rubinkowski, and the program's fearless leader, Patsy Sims.

I'm beyond thankful to the Overlook Press for all it has done for me—and it has done much, even outside the context of this book. Of course, this thanks is especially deserved by Peter Mayer, who championed my work when I thought it was all but lost, and who has spent his whole life in service of making good writing accessible to readers everywhere. This is not to diminish the roles of the other people who work at this lovely little press and who helped with this book, most notably Liese Mayer, Theresa Collier, Tracy Carns, George Davidson, and Jill Lichtenstadter. Thanks to Amanda Bartlett, Anthony Morais, and Mia Nolting for the beautiful cover design.

Over the course of my illness, I was blessed to meet many professionals—therapists, psychiatrists, nurses, and psychiatric technicians—who were kind, intelligent, and serious. One of these clinicians was Dr. Fern Klapper, who passed away in 2004. To them, I owe nothing short of my life.

I also met a number of very courageous and inherently special people who struggled with eating disorders. Many of them made it out alive, but in the process of researching this book, I've discovered that some did not. I'd like to add to the list of those to remember Ms. Kristie Duke and Ms. Stacy Musenga. Rest in peace.

I have to pause for a moment to recognize my ballast in life and love, Matthew Levy, who helps in many ways just by being himself.

Lastly, I reiterate my boundless affection and admiration for the people to whom this book is dedicated. I'll say "I love you" again, and again, and again . . .

SELECTED BIBLIOGRAPHY

THE FOLLOWING TEXTS HAVE BEEN IMMENSELY HELPFUL TO me over the course of writing this book:

Alcoholics Anonymous World Services. *Alcoholics Anonymous: Fourth Edition*. New York: Alcoholics Anonymous World Services, Inc., 2001.

American Psychiatric Association. *Diagnostic and Statistical Manual of Mental Disorders: DSM-V*. 5th ed. Washington, DC: American Psychiatric Association, 2013.

Barthelme, Donald. "Alice." In *Sixty Stories*. New York: Penguin Classics, 1982.

Baumann, Valerie. "'Wannarexic' Girls Yearn to Be Anorexic." USAToday.com, August 4, 2007. http://www.usatoday .com/news/health/2007-08-04-wannarexic_N.htm.

Becker, Ernest. *The Denial of Death*. New York: The Free Press, 1973.

Bruch, Hilde. *The Golden Cage: The Enigma of Anorexia Nervosa*. Cambridge: Harvard University Press, 1978.

Brumberg, Joan Jacobs. *Fasting Girls: The History of Anorexia Nervosa*. New York: Vintage, 2000.

Carr, David. *The Night of the Gun: A Reporter Investigates the Darkest Story of His Life; His Own*. New York: Simon & Schuster, 2008.

Didion, Joan. "The White Album." In *The Best American Essays of the Century*, ed. Joyce Carol Oates. New York: Houghton Mifflin, 2000.

Fagles, Robert, trans. *The Aeneid*. New York: Viking, 2006.

Frame, Janet. *An Autobiography*. New York: George Braziller, Inc., 1991.

Freud, Sigmund. "Analysis of a Phobia in a Five-Year-Old Boy." In *The Pelican Freud Library, Volumes 1–12*, edited by Angela Richards and translated by James Strachey. Vol. 8, Case Histories 1. New York: Pelican, 1975.

Gottlieb, Lori. *Stick Figure: A Diary of My Former Self*. New York: Simon & Schuster, 2000.

Greenfield, Lauren. *Thin*. San Francisco: Chronicle Books, 2006.

Hornbacher, Marya. *Wasted: A Memoir of Anorexia and Bulimia*. New York: HarperCollins, 1998.

Kalm, Leah M., and Richard D. Semba. "They Starved So That Others Be Better Fed: Remembering Ancel Keys and the

Minnesota Experiment." *The American Society for Nutritional Sciences Journal of Nutrition* 135 (June 2005): 1347–1352.

Kaysen, Susanna. *Girl, Interrupted.* New York: Turtle Bay Books, 1993.

Kolodny, Nancy. *When Food's a Foe: How You Can Confront and Conquer Your Eating Disorder.* New York: Little, Brown, 1998.

Krasnow, Michael. *My Life as a Male Anorexic.* Binghamton: Haworth Press, 1996.

Levenkron, Steven. *The Best Little Girl in the World.* New York: Warner Books, 1978.

Merkin, Daphne. "A Journey Through Darkness—My Life with Chronic Depression." *The New York Times Magazine,* May 6, 2009.

Pollan, Michael. *The Botany of Desire: A Plant's-Eye View of the World.* New York: Random House, 2001.

Reaves, Jessica. "Anorexia Goes High Tech." *Time,* July 31, 2001. http://www.time.com/time/health/article/0,8599,169660,00.html.

Taylor, Kate, ed. *Going Hungry: Writers on Desire, Self-Denial, and Overcoming Anorexia.* New York: Anchor Books, 2008.

Udovitch, Mim. "The Way We Live Now: 9-8-02: Phenomenon; A Secret Society of the Starving." *New York Times,* September 8, 2002. http://www.nytimes.com /2002/09 /08/magazine/the-way-we-live-now-9-8-02-phenomenon

-a-secret-society-of-the-starving.html?sec=&spon=&
pagewanted=all.

Wolf, Naomi. *The Beauty Myth: How Images of Beauty Are Used Against Women*. New York: Anchor Books, 1992.

ABOUT THE AUTHOR

Kᴇʟsᴇʏ Osɢᴏᴏᴅ is a Brooklyn-based writer. She has contributed to *The New Yorker*'s Culture Desk blog, *Salon*,
New York, and Gothamist, among other publications. She
also regularly blogs for *Psychology Today*. She is a graduate
of Columbia University and Goucher College's MFA program in Creative Nonfiction. *How to Disappear Completely*
is her first book.